THE TEACHER OF THE MENTALLY RETARDED

THE JOHN DAY SPECIAL EDUCATION BOOKS

For Teachers, Professional Workers and Parents of Retarded Children

SING AND LEARN: Simple Songs and Rhythms That Retarded Children Can Enjoy While Learning Basic Lessons
John W. Antey

GUIDING THE RETARDED CHILD: An Approach to a Total Education Program
Bernice B. Baumgartner

READINESS AND READING FOR THE RETARDED CHILD: A Teachers' Manual and Two Workbooks
Bebe Bernstein

THE CHILD WHO NEVER GREW
Pearl S. Buck

THE GIFTS THEY BRING: Our Debt to the Mentally Retarded
Pearl S. Buck and Gweneth T. Zarfoss

THE TEACHER OF THE MENTALLY RETARDED: A Guide to Careers in Special Education—Challenges, Demands, Rewards
Leon Charney and Edward LaCrosse

WHEN A CHILD IS DIFFERENT: A Basic Guide for Parents and Friends of Mentally Retarded Children, Giving Practical Suggestions on Their Education and Training
Maria Egg

TEACHING ARITHMETIC TO SLOW LEARNERS AND RETARDED
Abraham Feingold

BASIC LESSONS FOR RETARDED CHILDREN: A Workbook in Academic Skills and Holidays
Lucy Hamilton

TEACHING THE RETARDED CHILD TO TALK
Julia S. Molloy

TRAINABLE CHILDREN: Curriculum and Procedures
Julia S. Molloy

For Children with Reading Problems

STORIES FOR FUN AND ADVENTURE: High-Interest Reading Material for Reluctant Readers
Phyllis Fenner and Mary McCrea

MORE STORIES FOR FUN AND ADVENTURE: A Second Collection of Stories for Reluctant Readers
Phyllis Fenner and Mary McCrea

READING FUNDAMENTALS FOR TEEN-AGERS: A Workbook for Basic Reading Skill
Rose G. Neufeld

THE TEACHER OF THE MENTALLY RETARDED

LEON CHARNEY, Ph.D.
Director, Center for Special Education
Hofstra University

AND

EDWARD LaCROSSE, Ed.D.
Chairman, Department of Special Education
Newark State College

THE JOHN DAY COMPANY

Published by The John Day Company, Inc., 62 West 45th Street, New York, N.Y. 10036, and simultaneously in Canada by Longmans Canada Limited, Toronto.

Library of Congress Catalogue Card Number: 65-10918

MANUFACTURED IN THE UNITED STATES OF AMERICA

Second Impression

Contents

Introduction

At this very moment, thousands of young men and women in high schools and colleges across our nation are engaged in selecting a profession to which their lives will be dedicated. Perhaps you are one of them. In the four decades since 1920, there has been a dramatic shift in the selection of careers by young men and women from the areas of production to the areas of service to mankind. This development is, in part, a manifestation of the maturation of our democratic society; a society in which the youth continue to provide the vigor and vitality essential to our nation's growth. That a career dedicated to service to mankind should attract the youth of our nation is not surprising. Historically, young men and women have always been in the forefront of social change, have always been a source of dynamic energy leading to the realization of the noblest ideals.

In ever-increasing numbers, young people, motivated by the desire to participate in social change leading to the creation of a better world, are finding personal and professional satisfaction in careers of service to exceptional children. Nowhere has this been more dramatically demonstrated than in the education of the mentally retarded. The nobility of purpose motivating the young people desirous of entering the profession of education of the mentally retarded is embodied in the application statement of one student at a college in New Jersey. A sophomore and a recipient of an award for outstanding scholarship, this student applied for admission into the program of rigorous training leading to certification as a teacher of mentally retarded children in the state of New Jersey. Here is her statement:

I first became interested in entering the area of education of the mentally retarded earlier this semester after visiting the George Morris School for educable children in Bloomfield. Since the first visit, I have made two other visits in which I have observed and helped in one of the classes. During one of these times, I also had the opportunity to observe a class of six trainable children.

Before observing these children I had thought that I would not be able to work with them because I pictured them as being disfigured and uncoordinated. Now, however, I see that in appearance, for the most part, they seem almost normal. More important, I see that they are capable of learning to some degree, and that they have the same needs and wants as normal children, perhaps to a much greater extent than do normal children.

It is difficult for me to say in words exactly what my reason is for wanting to teach these children. Perhaps it can be better described as an intense feeling I have about them, a feeling I do not have to as great a degree about normal children. Although it is very important for normal children to grow and to mature physically and mentally, it is just as important, if not more so, that retarded children be helped to do this; since they will never reach the capacities of the average child, every effort should be made to enable them at least to reach their individual capacities and limitations.

This area of specialization offers an immense challenge, and I feel that I want and need to accept that challenge, in order to fulfill my own purpose in being a teacher. I realize that there are many disappointments and problems involved, but I feel certain that the rewards are well worth the effort.

In closing I will say simply that I care very much about these children, and that I want to be able to help them, not only in order to enable them to adjust as far as possible to their environment, but also to enable me to find purpose and enrichment in my own life.

The demands of such young men and women for opportunities to receive the training needed in this field has resulted in a rapid growth in the number of colleges and universities offering programs in the field of education of the mentally retarded. Thus, from twenty-two colleges offering training programs in 1949, a survey in 1963 revealed more than 190 colleges and universities offering programs in the training of prospective teachers of the mentally retarded.

At national, state and local levels, an increasing amount of effort is being expended on behalf of the more than five million mentally retarded persons in the United States. The neglect of these millions, so long a blot upon our philosophic commitment to the provision of equal opportunity for all, is an area of weakness which our democratic society is no longer willing to tolerate. That the area of education of the mentally retarded is one requiring the vigor and idealism of young men and women is implicit in the statement by the late John F. Kennedy, President of the United States:

> ... we as a nation have for too long postponed an intensive search for solutions to the problems of the mentally retarded. That failure should be corrected. ... The present shortage of personnel is a major problem in our logistics. More physicians, nurses, social workers, educators, psychologists, and other trained workers are needed.

Implicit also in this statement is a recognition that, as participants in the broad social movement having as its goal the realization of our democratic heritage in reference to the retarded, young people entering this field are crucial members of a professional team facilitating such change. The intimate contact with fields of medicine, psychology, and social work which characterizes the work of a teacher of mentally retarded children provides unlimited opportunities for professional and personal growth.

The vigor and creativity of young men and women like yourself are transforming the field of education of the mentally retarded from one of neglect to one of leadership in the total structure of education in our society. That this idealism and nobility of purpose can and do find expression in the field of education of the mentally retarded was demonstrated during the 1960 White House Conference on Children and Youth. From across the length and breadth of the United States men and women concerned with the education of the mentally retarded resolved that:

> If we believe deeply and thoroughly in children and if, as a profession, we believe deeply and thoroughly in education, we, as a "Society of the Concerned" are going to make a signifi-

cant contribution to mentally handicapped children and youth in the decade ahead.

To those of you who wish to become members of "The Society of the Concerned" this book is dedicated.

L. C.
E. L.

THE TEACHER OF THE MENTALLY RETARDED

CHAPTER 1

A Teacher Meets Her Class

First to greet her was Billy. His voice echoed through the corridor as he thundered down the hallway shouting, "Teacher, teacher, I'm back." His unkempt hair, unbuttoned coat, unlaced shoes and hot perspiring body left no doubt that this was Billy. Loving but hard to love, tender but aggressive, wanting attention but not knowing how to get it, Billy once again gave evidence of his desperate desire to be wanted and needed as he shouted, "Teacher, may I get the milk?" and dropped his well-worn hat and coat on the floor beside his desk.

In spite of the fact that it was her third year of teaching, Caroline Jameston had fidgeted nervously in anticipation of the clang of the admission bell. Now, chuckling at Billy's breathless greeting, her tension left her. Another school year had begun.

Throughout the city of Credo, the schools throbbed with activity. Deserted during the summer months, the buildings once again came to life and resounded to the orderly confusion of opening day. Many of the school buildings were new, reflecting the rapid growth of the city of Credo. The one hundred thousand citizens of this midwestern community were proud of the rapid growth of their city. The signs of this growth were readily visible; from the increasing number of suburban tracts to the long lines of children seeking their first admission to Credo's schools.

The citizens of Credo, like their counterparts in cities throughout the United States, take particular pride in their school system. Aware that the continuing growth of their community and their nation requires ever higher levels of education, the citizens of Credo have viewed their schools as a lifeline to the future. Central High, the original high school in Credo, has traditionally sent a large percentage of its student body on to the State College. As the city has grown, and three new high schools have been placed in operation in the suburban areas, Central High has witnessed a decline in the number of students going on for higher education. The exodus of middle and upper middle class families from the city to the suburbs has altered the composition of the student body at Central High. The concentration of minority groups and unskilled workers in the older sections of the city has changed not only Central High, but the older elementary schools as well.

As these changes occurred, teachers in the schools in the older sections of the city became increasingly alarmed at the number of children who were unable to keep up with work at their grade levels. Many of these boys and girls were two or more years below grade level in academic achievement and appeared restless and unhappy in school.

Nor were the newer sections of the city free from educational problems. Some children had never been permitted to enter the schools of Credo because of their obvious retardation. The parents of these children joined together to form the Credo Association for Retarded Children, and for many years operated classes for their children in the basement of a local church. The continuous request of the Credo Association for Retarded Children for the public schools to assume responsibility for the education of their children, combined with the concern of teachers in the older sections of the city over the growing number of school failures, resulted in the establishment of special classes for mentally retarded children. Today in Credo there are forty special education classes for the 596 mildly retarded pupils and twelve special classes for 95 moderately retarded pupils.

Caroline Jameston is a teacher in one of the classes for mildly retarded pupils. Since the boys and girls in her class were capable of eventually attaining an academic achievement level of fourth–fifth grade, they were considered to be "educable" children. Because they needed a great deal of individual attention, the class size was restricted to no more than fifteen. Ranging in age from nine to thirteen, Caroline Jameston's children had in common the bitter experience of failure in the regular elementary grades; failure stemming from their retarded rate of learning.

She intercepted Billy as he attempted, shoelaces flying, to exit from the classroom and complete his quest for milk from the school cafeteria. Led gently but firmly to the jumble created by his hat and coat on the floor, Billy grinned sheepishly as he recalled last year's many lessons on "how to hang up clothing." Billy—resident of seven foster homes in as many years—at the age of ten took great pride in his newly found ability to write his first and last name.

Ralph and Wayne entered the classroom simultaneously and in silence. With studied deliberation they ignored her warm greeting and surveyed the classroom with a sneer. In the course of their two years in the special class they had moved from bitter rejection to a grudging acceptance of Miss Jameston, the classroom and the school. Two outcasts pitted against the world, they were inseparable. Crude wooden guns fashioned from the end of an apple crate protruded from their back pockets—guns that symbolized their determination to strike back at a world that had treated them with such cruelty. Ralph's shoulders still bore the black and blue marks of his father's last beating, and Wayne could never recall having had a father. In unison Wayne and Ralph hung their jackets in the closet, and still without speaking, wandered to the window and stared out at the rapidly emptying school yard.

The fluttering of Sally's fingers as they clutched at Miss Jameston's dress was a signal of her chronic distress. Kneeling quickly, Miss Jameston clutched the girl to her and waited for the tremors to subside. She noted with satisfaction that it was taking Sally less and less time to overcome her hypersensitive reaction to the movement and noises all about her. This scene would be repeated many times in the coming year as Sally learned to control her excessive response to stimulation. In a few moments Sally stepped back and with a smile said, "Hello, Miss Jameston."

With her hand resting lightly on Sally's shiny blond hair, Miss Jameston guided her to the desk in the screened corner of the room. Sally would need a period of quiet before starting the day's activities. Indeed, it was understood that she could go to her "quiet office" whenever she felt the need during the school day.

The encephalitis which had stricken Sally when she was six had come close to taking her life. As it was, she remained in a coma for six months. Finally up and about, she was very different from the quiet, well-mannered child she had been before the disease. She was constantly talking, constantly moving, prone to accidents and to violent shifts in mood. Only in Miss Jameston's special class had she found the understanding and skillful teaching she needed to help her adjust to the confusion and distortion resulting from the injury to her brain.

Clean and starched, wearing far too many crinkly petticoats under her scarlet dress, eleven-year-old Donna entered the room with exaggerated coyness and artificial shyness and presented Miss Jameston with a bouquet of flowers. With a smile and a simple, "Why thank you, Donna," Miss Jameston accepted the gift. She knew that Donna's constant quest for signs of love and affection was her way of disguising the self-doubt and confusion she felt when any demands were made upon her. Her mother and father devoted considerable money and energy in the attempt to fill Donna's endless need for new clothes and toys; items which provided Donna with at least a transitory reassurance of her personal worth. So great was her insecurity that Donna frequently pitted one child against another so that she could report their infractions to the teacher and consequently shine by contrast.

As Miss Jameston adjusted the flowers in the vase, Donna, making sure that Ralph's eyes were upon her, twirled about with a great rustling of petticoats. Turning with a dazzling smile, she asked Ralph if she could have his place by the window. Face reddening, Ralph moved silently aside.

Harvey entered the room next, his school-patrol belt displayed prominently across his chest. He returned Miss Jameston's smile of greeting and in a well-modulated voice said, "Good morning, Teacher. We took good care of the children on the bus this morning. Boy, I'm glad that we're back at school again. Will I get to be school patrol again this year?" Without waiting for her reply he stooped and picked up a crayon which had fallen to the floor and returned it to Miss Jameston's desk. He acknowledged her thank you with a polite "You're welcome" and wandered over to the table to examine the still-empty fish tank.

His movements indicated that he had no doubts about his ability to handle the many tasks which needed doing to put the classroom in order, and that he wanted to get on with the work. One of four mentally retarded children in the same family, Harvey was a solid citizen whose paper route and weekend lawn mowing and snow shoveling business did much to supplement the family's meager income.

With studious care, Harvey unscrewed the cover to the fish tank air pump and carefully oiled the tiny cylinder. Miss Jameston turned away to hide her grin. Machinery fascinated Harvey and on numerous occasions he had gently displaced Miss Jameston in her attempts to master the tape recorder, the motion picture projector and other items of equipment. In anything pertaining to machinery, Harvey was more competent than most boys of thirteen. Yet, subtraction caused him to furrow his brow in bewilderment, and he would never master the complexities of long division or read with understanding beyond the fourth grade level. But when the custodial staff needed assistance, they called Harvey, for his willingness to help and his ability to handle machinery had made a lasting impression. When it came to cars, machines and people, Harvey knew his way about the world. When it came to reading, writing, arithmetic and spelling, Harvey was lost.

Richard almost exploded into the classroom. Grasping Miss Jameston's arm with both hands, the words poured out, "Good morning, Miss Jameston, when do we start feeding the fish? I went to camp this summer and I got a new bicycle and my brother fell down and broke his arm and I'm glad to be back at school and when can . . ." Miss Jameston interrupted in midstream with a quiet, "Good morning, Richard, won't you please go and hang up your hat and coat now?" "Oh yes, Teacher, I be glad . . . Hi Ralph, Hi Billy, Hi Harvey. . . ." The desks seemed to leap from his path as he made his way to the coat closet, an ever increasing amount of disarray in his wake. At Miss Jameston's somewhat frantic, "Richard, *the desks!*" he turned, grief at the implied reprimand starting across his face.

How to contain this little bundle of explosive energy within the confines of a 30 by 30 classroom was one of Caroline Jameston's chronic problems, particularly since this bundle of energy was sensitive and could sulk for the entire morning if not reassured. At the age of nine Richard, when working up to his capacity, could barely achieve at the first grade level, and even here his short attention span made any instruction extremely difficult.

With Miss Jameston's help the desks were quickly straightened and Richard reassured. He ricocheted up to Harvey who, without a word but with a heavy sigh of resignation, handed Richard the oil can. Richard *had* to be kept busy, and Harvey knew it!

The grease on John's face complemented the oil stains on David's clothing. The two brothers, aged thirteen and twelve respectively, entered the classroom bearing evidence of their early morning activities in the yard full of wrecked cars that constituted the lawn area of their home. John's right hand clutched the remains of the speedometer which he had brought to school for disassembling. "Hi! You got screwdriver?" "*A* screwdriver," said Miss Jameston, as she reached for her desk drawer. "Oh—good," said John as he divested himself of his hat and coat, took his seat, and prepared to attack the speedometer.

David's "hi" was casual. Without any further ado, he pulled a chair close to John and watched his brother.

Last to enter the room was Myrna, the oldest girl in the class, leading Eddy by the hand, clutching his lunch pail along with hers. The tone of her greeting to Miss Jameston implied that they were colleagues in the profession of taking care of the little kids. She led Eddy into the room where she took off his coat and hung it up for him, and then seated him at his seat before putting her own coat away. During all this she kept up a constant stream of remarks: "Oh brother, I really have to take care of you. Here! Let me do that for you." Eddy, the youngest in the class, very passively allowed Myrna to do everything for him. Timid and withdrawn, he would not speak unless it was absolutely necessary. By the end of last year he had developed the habit of looking at Myrna whenever he was asked a question by Miss Jameston.

Myrna was the most capable student in the class academically, but in many other ways, the most dependent of all Caroline Jameston's children. Only in a non-competitive environment and in relationship to a child with ability less than her own did Myrna feel the necessary strength for her to face the school day. Yet, her intellectual ability, far below the norm three years ago, had climbed steadily and revealed a potential for return to the regular grades. Building the confidence necessary in order to return to the regular class was Caroline Jameston's primary goal for Myrna.

The final bell rang. A new school year was under way.

CHAPTER 2

A Day in the Special Class

As the sound of the bell faded, Caroline Jameston turned and faced the class. It was the anticipation of this moment that had caused her to devote a considerable portion of her time over the summer vacation to the development of the plan book which lay open on her desk. Yet, in spite of the fact that the plan book contained a detailed and thoughtful guide to this day, it was already evident from the behavior of the children that the plan needed revision. Established routine called for the children to be at their desks upon the ringing of the final bell. Today, however, most of the children were gathered around Harvey at the fish tank and a lively discussion was in progress regarding the type of fish to be placed in the tank. A smaller group had gathered around John's desk and was observing with rabid attention the dissection of the speedometer.

Miss Jameston walked slowly to the group around the fish tank and casually entered into the discussion. It would be unwise, she knew, both in reference to the momentary problem of getting the children to their seats and in reference to the broader problem of attaining a successful school day, to simply order a halt to their activities. Since they were so interested in the fish tank, why not encourage and utilize that interest? In addition, she was very much aware that in the past many of her children had felt the sting of commands abruptly and impatiently given.

The small class size and her awareness of special needs of her children enabled Caroline Jameston to move quickly to capitalize on the interest and motivation she recognized in the group around the fish tank. There would be many hundreds of times in the course of the coming year when she would undertake to build upon the spontaneous interest of the class in all aspects of the world in which they lived.

"Well," she said, addressing the group, "what shall we do first?" There was a moment of silence and then Harvey, with the air of a man whose patience was sorely tried by the confusion about him, responded, "We'll have to put the sand and water in. That's the first thing." Billy, his face flushed with excitement, grabbed for the fish tank, swung around and shouted at the top of his lungs, "I wanna do it! Gimme it!"

A dozen hands reached for the fish tank. The group that had been involved in the dissection of the speedometer joined the group at the table and all were clamoring for the right to fill the tank and care for the fish. The voices were becoming argumentative as each asserted his claim.

"Now just a moment!" Her voice, clear and sharp and tinged with indignation, brought immediate silence to the group. More gently, now that she had their attention, she continued, "Boys and girls, we *do* have many things to do today, don't we? It's going to be fun to set up our fish tank, and each one of you will have your very own fish.

But, it wouldn't be fair if I just said, 'Harvey, you're in charge,' or 'Sally, you're in charge.' Why wouldn't it be fair?" She had the attention of the entire group now as they stood clustered around the table containing the fish tank. "It wouldn't be fair 'cause *I* wanna do it," said Billy, missing the point. "Oh, yeah," snarled Ralph, jabbing Billy with his elbow. "It wouldn't be fair 'cause *I* wanna have *my* chance!" Myrna, with an angry glance at Billy and Ralph, in a voice brimming with disgust, remarked, "Well, we sure better sit down and talk about it or we'll be standing around here till it's time to go home!" The laughter which greeted this remark broke the mounting tension, and at Miss Jameston's nod of approval the boys and girls returned to their seats.

With more formality than she had yet displayed, Caroline Jameston addressed the class from the center of the room: "I am happy to see all of you, and I know that there are many things that you want to do today. You want very much to fill the fish tank, and I know you want to talk about what you did over the summer. But you just saw what happens when everyone wants to do everything all at once. Everything gets all mixed up." Stepping to the chalkboard, she wrote the date, and once again facing the class asked, "Just what *are* some of the things we have to do today?"

"Fill the fish tank!" shrieked Billy, preparing to leap from his seat. "Billy, I am so sorry." Caroline Jameston's voice quivered with pain and disappointment. "Boys and girls," she said sadly, "what is it that Billy has forgotten to do? His answer is a good one, but what is it that he has forgotten to do?" Donna's hand was raised. In her most ladylike manner, Donna pointed out that Billy had forgotten to raise his hand. "Billy," said Miss Jameston, "why do we have to do that?" Crestfallen, Billy hung his head and refused to answer. "Boys and girls, why do we have to raise our hands?" John's answer was clear and to the point, "So we don't get all mixed up like we did with the fish tank." "Right, John," said Miss Jameston moving to Billy's desk and resting her hand gently on his head. "Now, Billy, what's one thing we want to do today?"

Billy's struggle was a silent one . . . to punish Miss Jameston for her reprimand by refusing to answer, or to cooperate and reap the reward of her praise. The seconds ticked by. Slowly raising his hand, but with still lowered head Billy replied in a barely audible voice, "We've gotta fill the fish tank." "Right, Billy!" exclaimed Miss Jameston. "And Billy, thank you so much for raising your hand." Billy lifted his head and beamed.

Turning back to the chalkboard, she wrote "fill fish tank" under the date. "Is there anything else we must do?" she queried. Every hand in the room was raised. "Flag salute," said Harvey. "Take the roll," said David. Quickly, Caroline Jameston listed the comments under the date, adding those areas which the children omitted. When the list was completed, the discussion shifted to the *order* with which each item should be undertaken. There was general agreement that the flag salute should come first and that the filling of the fish tank (much to Billy's chagrin) would have to be undertaken later in the day. With a pleased smile, she pointed out to the group that what they had done was devise a "schedule" of the day's activities; that a schedule was like a plan for the day, and that this would help to avoid the kind of mix-up that had taken place earlier.

"Harvey," said Miss Jameston, "would you please lead us in the flag salute?" The class was silent for the formal opening of the school day. Harvey left his seat, moved to the front of the room and with great dignity and pride lifted the flag from the socket in the wall, carried it to the center of the room and stood at attention. The class stood at his order and placing their hands on their hearts, recited the Pledge of Allegiance.

As Harvey returned the flag to its place, Myrna was called upon to read the second item on the schedule and to undertake the completion of a large attendance chart which hung conspicuously, but until this moment unnoticed, by the door. The chart consisted of a series of questions with spaces for the insertion of cards bearing the answers to the questions. The attention of the group was focused on the chart now, as Myrna undertook to read the first question. Her face was flushed, and her voice quivered a bit as she was confronted with the task which had been for her a source of constant failure and chronic embarrassment—the task of reading. Many times in the past Myrna had seen a teacher turn away in disgust as she stumbled through reading material, four years behind the rest of her class. It had taken Caroline Jameston more than seven months of intensive work with Myrna to help her attain the confidence necessary to stand before the group and read. Myrna read the first sentence, "Today is" and selected the appropriate response card and held it up in front of the group. Billy's hand shot up as Myrna paused, waiting for the remainder of the class to read the card that she held, and respond to it. Face flushed, hand waving, "School!" shouted Billy, and the class roared with laughter. When the laughter subsided, Miss Jameston, still chuckling at Billy's enthusiasm, remarked, "You are absolutely right, Billy, today is 'school,' but what is the word on the card?"

With much hesitation Myrna worked her way through the remaining questions on the chart, questions which Caroline Jameston could have completed by herself in a few moments. However, her concern throughout the school day would be with the attempt to involve all of the children in the activities of the class. For Myrna, the use of the attendance chart helped her to overcome her fear of reading. For Billy, the attendance chart provided the opportunity to participate, even though he could not read. For the entire class, the completion of the attendance chart, like the development of the "schedule," meant that words and numbers were being utilized in a meaningful sense. The use of such a chart also was an attempt to help the children to overcome the serious deficiencies in understanding time and number concepts. Harvey, despite his thirteen years of chronological age, still could not recall his birthday. Billy had no useful conception of such abstractions as day of the week and month of the year. And while John could dissect a speedometer, neither he nor any member of the class had a working grasp of the meaning of "mile."

Quietly, Donna asked whether she could copy the information on the attendance chart onto the formal attendance report which was to be returned to the main office of the school. Miss Jameston nodded and Donna, her face reflecting her eagerness to have the opportunity to go to the main office, proceeded to copy the necessary information. Donna completed the task quietly and left for the office. A few minutes after the door closed behind her, Miss Jameston walked quietly to the telephone and called the office to notify them that Donna was on her way. Miss Jameston was well aware of Donna's proclivity for flirtation, and this was a necessary precaution. It was precisely because Donna had difficulty in fulfilling responsibility that Caroline Jameston entrusted her with the attendance report. Donna would learn—but only by being given the opportunity to make mistakes!

Without being told, Wayne distributed a printed sheet to each child in the room. The children took up their pencils and began to work at the assigned task. This task, so much a matter of routine that instructions were no longer necessary, entailed the completion of a series of questions which Miss Jameston had gleaned from employment service job-application forms. Richard would only be able to print his first and last name. Sally, on the other hand, was able to write the answers to five questions concerning her name, address, date and place of birth. Myrna could complete sixteen questions, including questions dealing with her mother's name and father's name, age, previous place of residence, etc. The ability to promptly and accurately respond to questions of this nature reduced embarrassment and increased the likelihood of future employment. Such training was a vital aspect of the curriculum for Caroline Jameston's children.

She moved among the students as they worked, assisting and encouraging. In the short space of forty-five minutes since the opening of the school day, the class had engaged in four distinct activities. This abundance of activities was necessary, for it was difficult for her children to stay for any protracted length of time with a single task. Because of their poor learning skills, because they anticipated failure, the boys and girls in Miss Jameston's class exhibited an attention span far below that of intellectually normal boys and girls of the same age. In order for Caroline Jameston to treat the class as a group and keep them involved and interested, it was necessary for her to plan a large number of activities, some of which would be conducted simultaneously. She also knew that it would be necessary to vary the nature of the activities so that periods of relative inaction, like reading, would be followed by periods of greater activity with the opportunity for the children to move about and talk. This morning had been going well and her class was functioning as a cohesive group.

Suddenly Wayne jumped from his seat, crumpled his paper, and stomping to the front of the room flung the paper into the wastebasket. His face wore an expression of complete and open defiance. As he slammed himself back into his chair, Miss Jameston paused for a moment and then moved quickly to Wayne's side. The rage which emanated from Wayne was almost a tangible thing. Placing her hand on Wayne's shoulder, she softly asked, "What's the matter, Wayne?" Wayne blurted back, "You didn't help me!" "I'm sorry, Wayne." Caroline Jameston was aware that the help which Wayne was seeking had nothing to do with the assignment that he was to complete. Wayne had completed many identical assignments and his call for help was an expression of pain at the frustration and loneliness of his life. "You didn't help me," repeated Wayne. "You didn't help me, and nobody helps me, nobody ever helps me, and I don't give a damn, and I'm not going to do it because nobody ever helps me." The tears ran down Wayne's cheeks and the heads of the other children turned in his direction. The fingers of her hand gently caressed Wayne's shoulder as she softly said, "I'll help you, Wayne," and putting a chair close to Wayne's desk, seated herself near him. Without a word, Harvey brought another assignment sheet and placed it on Wayne's desk. Nothing more was said. Secure in the knowledge that a woman who cared for him was close by, Wayne finished the assignment, his teacher by his side, her hand resting on his shoulder.

One at a time the boys and girls in the class brought their completed assignments to her. The familiar routine and the familiar freedom which the children had in the past experienced in the special class was manifested as they completed their assignment. While Miss Jameston concerned herself with an individual review of each child's work, the boys and girls moved, as their interests took them, to individual and small group activities. Two or three children gathered at the game table set up in one area of the room and proceeded to become involved in a simple card game. A few others gravitated to the library area of the room where they quickly became engrossed in the Sears Roebuck catalogues prominently displayed on the library table. Others worked at the art area of the room, mixing paints in preparation for the day's activity.

Billy's face reflected his hurt and confusion as Miss Jameston with great gentleness pointed out his misspelling of his last name. Myrna bubbled with pride as Miss Jameston, using her most brilliant red pencil, scrawled a "100%, excellent" across Myrna's paper. Harvey tried to hide his disappointment as a correction was made of his erroneous response to the question dealing with his date of birth. Donna returned before the completion of the discussions over the individual papers. She had missed the assignment, but in her case, the development of a sense of responsibility was of primary importance and the experience of a successful trip to the office and return was a step in that direction.

As Miss Jameston completed the last paper she paused and surveyed the room. The boys and girls, engaged as they were in a variety of activities, were conversing freely with each other. True, their voices were somewhat hushed. They were aware from previous experience that the opportunity to participate in these activities depended on their ability to refrain from causing undue disturbance. However, the class was by no means silent. She felt a quiet flush of pride as she perceived the children moving freely about the room, conversing freely, and yet manifesting a degree of control that held the noise at normal conversational level. The control was from within rather than from without, emanating from a sense of responsible freedom rather than from a teacher's force. It was by no means perfect (Donna and Billy and Wayne had much to learn), but it worked.

There was a flurry of activity as the children moved from the unsupervised free period to compliance with her request. Quickly, she moved from one group to another. At the paint table she called upon Harvey to remember to clean his paint brush before returning it to the paintbox. Wayne was reminded to clean the easel with a wet sponge. At the library corner she noted with pleasure that Billy had remembered to replace the books on the proper shelves. Instruction and supervision in such tasks as cleaning up after a work area had been used, in returning material to its proper place, in the necessity for cleanliness and order, occupied a prominent position in Miss Jameston's instructional goals for the children. It was no accident that many activities were available to the boys and girls. The special class was designed to confront the children with the *necessity* for cleanliness, order and routine.

The work areas cleaned and in proper order, the children resumed their seats. As the children seated themselves in a semicircle, Miss Jameston took from the closet a large sombrero and placing it on her head she turned to face the audience. Their laughter was spontaneous and prolonged and she joined in. With mock seriousness, Caroline Jameston asked, "What are you laughing about?" Eleven voices blurted, "Your funny hat!" "Where do people wear hats like this?" she asked. "Don't tell me though, don't tell me. But just think about it for a minute. If you think you know the answer, put up your hand. If you are right, I am going to let you go to the map and see if you can show me the place where people wear hats like the one I am wearing."

Hands waved excitedly. One by one Miss Jameston recognized the lofted hands and called them to her and listened to their whispered responses. Only Donna knew where the hat came from. However, although she was able to name the country from which the hat had come, when confronted with the request to locate Mexico on the map, Donna placed that country in the vicinity of Nova Scotia. "Well, you were right, Donna, the sombrero comes from Mexico, but Mexico is here, south of where we live," and Miss Jameston traced the outline of Mexico on the large wall map and pointed out its location in relationship to Credo. "Now, who can tell me where I spent my summer vacation?"

Every hand in the room shot up and turning to David, Miss Jameston said, "Okay, David, where did I spend my vacation?" Quietly David replied, "Mexico—do you know where I spent mine?" "No," said Miss Jameston, "where did you spend your vacation, David, and what did you do?"

Before David could answer she turned to Ralph and instructed him to go to the board and write a summary of each child's description of his summer vacation. Ralph, proud of his ability to spell, stepped to the board and wrote "Miss Jameston went to Mexico."

"Now, David," said Miss Jameston, "what did you do?"

"I stayed home and went swimming," replied David. Ralph wrote "David went swimming." One by one the boys and girls were given the opportunity to report briefly on the highlights of their summer vacation. When Wayne's turn came he launched into a lengthy description of the voyage which he had taken on his father's cabin cruiser and of his adventures during the trip with pirates who attempted to rob the boat. Teacher and children listened patiently, entertained by Wayne's story but well aware that it had been years since Wayne had seen his father and that Wayne himself was residing in a foster home from which he escaped only by these flights of fancy. "Did you go swimming, Wayne?" asked Miss Jameston, when he had concluded. "Yes, I went swimming every day," replied Wayne. Turning to Ralph she instructed him to write "Wayne went swimming this summer."

When each of the children had the opportunity to briefly describe and have recorded the highlights of his summer vacation, Caroline Jameston drew a red chalk square around the sentences. The red square indicated that this material was to be saved and used during the week in the classroom newspaper. This class newspaper was a highlight of her reading program. It drove home to the children the importance of reading. It was highly motivating material since it concerned the children and their activities. The sentences enclosed by the red band would also be copied into the notebooks of those children who could read and write. Drawings would be made to illustrate each story. Thus the reading, spelling and writing would be based upon material drawn directly from the life experiences of the children.

Noting Billy's increasing restlessness, Miss Jameston turned to her desk and gave him the order slip for the milk. He quickly left the room for the cafeteria. She knew that Billy's attention span was the most limited of the group and that he could be held in conversation for only a short period of time before he lost interest. Consequently, she was prepared for Billy's restlessness and utilized his eagerness to be of assistance.

Glancing at the clock, she realized with a start that the morning was half gone and it was time for the "coffee break." It was a break which was eagerly awaited for reasons other than the need for relaxation. For many of the children this mid-morning break constituted breakfast. In addition to nourishment, the "coffee break" provided an opportunity for relaxed, informal discussion.

Since this was the first day of school, Miss Jameston assigned various tasks to the children to set up the dining table. She had already prepared the cinnamon toast and cookies which would be the main fare. In the course of the coming week, however, the establishment of a menu for the mid-morning break, the preparation of the food, and the responsibility for serving and cleaning would be formally established and duly assigned. Both boys and girls would participate in these activities, since every effort was made to train all of the children in these skills which would help them become independent adults.

Upon her request, the children pulled their chairs to the table. The noise and confusion mounted as the chairs were dragged across the floor. Caroline Jameston strode to the front of the room, her face flushed with annoyance, and her voice had a snap to it as she said, "Just stop where you are! No talking!"

The boys and girls froze in their tracks. "Just a minute," said Miss Jameston. "Now you are doing something wrong. You know better than this! Can anyone here tell me what's wrong?" The boys and girls looked at each other and Harvey blurted out, "The chairs."

"Right, Harvey," she nodded. "Now you know better than to drag your chairs across the floor. It seems to me that we are going to have to rehearse what I taught you last year. So bring your chairs back to the circle." Quietly the boys and girls did so. "Now look," she said, "does anybody here remember how we were supposed to carry a chair?" Donna volunteered to demonstrate the technique of grasping the chair from the rear and lifting it slightly from the floor and carrying it silently across the room. "All right," said Miss Jameston, "let's try it again." Quickly, with a minimum of confusion and noise, the chairs were carried to the table and properly placed. The quiet movement to the table was interrupted by Billy's clatter as he unsuccessfully tried to manipulate both the door knob and a dozen cartons of milk. Harvey quickly opened the door and relieved the hot and perspiring Billy of his burden.

There was silence as all were seated at the table. While the conversation would be informal, the procedure was well structured and quite formal. The insistence on formalities at this time was not capricious on Miss Jameston's part but was a vital aspect of the training in social skills so important in a program for the mentally retarded. With many a "please" and "thank you" the mid-morning "coffee break" was under way. The conversation was free and easy in an atmosphere of friendship. Even Ralph and

Wayne were observed to laugh at one of Harvey's wry comments.

Munching her cookie, Caroline Jameston reflected on the morning's activities. The remainder of the morning would be devoted to starting the science unit on "fishes" and plans for setting up the fish tank. After lunch would come music and craft activities.

Harvey caught her eye and grinned. "It's good to be back, isn't it, Miss Jameston?"

CHAPTER 3

The Teacher Visits

It was 4:10 by the time Caroline Jameston completed her revision of the plan for the next day. With a prideful glance about the classroom, she noted that it would not be necessary for the custodian to concern himself at any great length with the situation in her classroom. All the jobs had been done, and in spite of the multiplicity of the activities which had taken place during the day, the room was clean and orderly. She hurried now, down the corridors of the building, to her waiting automobile. Her working day was not completed with the children leaving school; there were home visits to be undertaken and she had planned one for this afternoon. Knowing that the retarded children in her class encountered a significantly greater degree of frustration and turmoil in their lives than did normal children, she undertook a minimum of two visits each year to the home of each of the children in her group. Only in this manner could she gain the degree of insight and understanding necessary for the success of her endeavor to help her children. These visits also provided an opportunity for Caroline Jameston to develop a cooperative program with the parents of the children in her class. She knew that the five hours a day that the children spent at school were only a fraction of their learning day. Progress at home or in school could be impeded through lack of mutual cooperation. She also knew that the activities presented in school must be made meaningful to the children. Only through contact with the home could she select units of work for development at school which would be related to the lives of her children. Further, since the activities undertaken by the special class often departed markedly from the curriculum of the regular grades, it was necessary that the parents have a clear understanding of the goals of the special class and the procedures employed to achieve those goals. Much careful work undertaken by Miss Jameston designed to build a sense of achievement and self-worth in the children could be undermined by excessive demands for academic achievement at home. These home visits were of importance not only in helping her understand her children; they were also important in that they represented an attempt to alter the child's environment outside of the school situation.

The black and blue streaks which she had noted on Ralph's arm were uppermost in Caroline Jameston's mind as she backed her car from the school driveway and pointed it in the direction of the oldest portion of the city. It was not by chance that she had selected Ralph's home for her first visit. She had attempted on two separate occasions during the previous year to visit Ralph's parents and on each occasion, although the appointment had been made and rescheduled, there had been no response to her ringing of the doorbell. Ralph was in trouble and Miss Jameston knew it. The scars on his body were poor indicators of the extent of the scars on his soul. His bitter silent withdrawal gave indication that the scars were truly deep and extensive. Driving almost mechanically, Miss Jameston could once again hear Ralph's shriek ringing in her ears. Last year, shortly before the closing of school, she had seen him on the playground surrounded by a group of older boys, his face flushed, his fists clenched and tears streaming down his face as he screamed, "My father's not a drunkard! He's not!" Little wonder that in the regular classes, prior to his coming to the special class, Ralph had been noted both for his habit of simply putting his head down on the desk and going to sleep and for his vicious battles on the school playground.

Deep in thought, Caroline Jameston realized with a start that she was approaching Ralph's home. Having hardly noticed the gradual change of the character of the city as she drove, the environment which now confronted her came as a jolt. The broken windows of the abandoned factory were stark reminders of the growing blight that characterized the old area in which Ralph lived. Next to the factory the rendering plant still functioned and a pall of foul-smelling dust filtered the sunlight and cast a grayish hue over the region. Spotted among the factory buildings, interspersed by vacant lots, heaped with the accumulated refuse of years of poor sanitation, were the clapboard homes of the residents of this area. At one time these homes had been owned by the meat-packing plant, whose shattered windows marked the demise of the original industry in Credo. The peeling paint and rotting timber of homes that had been built eighty-five years ago as temporary structures to house the workers in the packing plant underscored the air of age and decay that characterized the region and pointed up the long overdue need for renovation of this area. Garbage cans, overflowing and without covers, spilled their contents onto the sidewalks. A group of children using the garbage can covers as shields, laths as swords and empty tin cans as missiles were engaged in not-so-mock warfare on the corner of the block.

Driving with care to avoid the swarms of children and axle-breaking potholes that filled the roadway, Miss Jameston pulled her car up in front of Ralph's house, and with a quick flick of the ignition, turned to survey the scene. Set back from the sidewalk the path to the house was obscured by the knee-high weeds which grew in profusion. The front, rear and side of the house were littered with the decaying remains of outdated automobiles, parts of which were strewn on the porch, spread through the garage, and spilled over onto the weed-covered walk. Over the window of the front bedroom hung a blanket to replace the glass which had long since been broken out.

She stepped carefully on the broken steps as she climbed to the porch, then ducking under the filled clothesline, made her way to the door. The blaring voice of the television set was abruptly stilled with her knock. The sudden silence followed by the slight movement of the blanket over the window indicated to her that she was being observed; that although she had made an appointment it was questionable whether she would be allowed to enter. The question was resolved when Ralph came bounding up onto the front porch, greeted her and opened the door, catching his mother at her position by the window. For the first time in the year that Ralph had been in Miss Jameston's class, she was to meet one of his parents.

As she entered the house, the TV was turned on full blast by Ralph. Ralph's mother, though she invited Caroline Jameston in, went on with her activities, and the conversation was carried on as Miss Jameston followed Ralph's mother about the house. The interior of the house was notably bare with very few pieces of furniture. The missing wallpaper, the scarred moldings, the cracked linoleum served to reinforce the air of futility with which Ralph's mother faced the task of caring for seven children.

The first words uttered by Ralph's mother were "What did he do now?" Calmly explaining that Ralph had done nothing wrong and that she simply had wanted to meet his parents, Caroline Jameston pointed out that she visited the homes of all the children in her class. She was positive in her approach and friendly in her manner and kept the conversation oriented to the progress which Ralph had made in school. Noting that Ralph's mother was becoming increasingly anxious, Miss Jameston thanked her for permitting her to visit, and with a wave at Ralph, departed.

It was a beginning; a small step lasting all of fifteen minutes, and yet an extremely important step. Nothing had really been changed in Ralph's life, and yet something had been changed. The second visit would be easier. Ralph's mother now knew that Miss Jameston had come to help, not to criticize. This was probably the first visit which Ralph's mother had had from a professional person which was not judgmental in nature. Ralph's mother now knew that Miss Jameston's primary concern was for the welfare of Ralph.

Miss Jameston knew that the process of becoming accepted and trusted was a lengthy one. The gap between their two worlds was indeed wide. To Ralph's mother, Caroline Jameston represented authority, comparative wealth, discipline, control and learning. All of these things were foreign and threatening to Ralph's mother. Her life had been one of extreme poverty, brutality, and a constant struggle for survival. Her experience with persons of Caroline Jameston's social class had always been related to trouble; the social worker, the police, and the youth authority, had all appeared on the scene in response to difficulties. This was the very first time that a representative of authority had come merely to visit.

With a sigh, she drove rapidly from Ralph's home to her own apartment. It had been a busy day, indeed, and she realized with a start that she would have barely enough time to change and be on time for the dinner invitation which Donna's parents had extended to her. Confronting her wardrobe, she pondered the problem of the selection of a suitable dress for this occasion. It would have to be her very best, she knew, for Donna's parents occupied a position at the top of the social register in the city of Credo, and one simply did not go for dinner at their home wearing other than one's best.

The rambling colonial style house sat in the center of two immaculately manicured acres, surrounded by pine and fir. The spotless winding driveway led to the canopied entrance. Caroline Jameston was met at the door by the starched uniformed maid who addressed her by name and, quickly removing her coat, let her into the drawing room. With proper protocol the maid dismissed herself, and left to summon Donna's mother. In a little while the doors of the drawing room opened and she was greeted by Mr. and Mrs. Walker, and Donna. Her face flushed from the excitement of having her teacher visit her home, Donna glanced nervously at her father, awaiting the nod that would indicate to her that she was to handle the introductions. The nod came, accompanied by a certain grimness of expression, and Donna launched herself into the complexities of a formal introduction; a procedure which her parents had rehearsed with her many, many times. In a voice tense with fear over the possibility of error and the consequent commission of a social faux pas, Donna tremblingly, but successfully, completed the introductions. Following this, she dismissed herself and left the room. Protocol in her home called for children to be seen and heard only on certain occasions.

"How would you like your drink, Miss Jameston?" said Mr. Walker, moving with practiced skill about the bar. At her response, the refreshments were quickly served and Mr. and Mrs. Walker, seating themselves facing Miss Jameston, began an interrogation regarding Donna's progress in school. Their anxiety concerning the nature of Donna's academic achievement was evident, as they described with much pride the academic and social success of an older brother and sister. Behind their query Miss Jameston was aware of the reservoir of pain and disappointment with which both mother and father viewed Donna's retardation. Thus, although Donna was academically the most capable child in the class, her status in her own family was that of the most severely retarded. Donna faced major problems arising from the discrepancy between her family's expectations and hopes and her ability. The intensity of Donna's drive for acceptance, her flirtatiousness, her never-ending quest for love and affection, and her rejection of academic work in the class became much more understandable. Understandable also was the frequent failure on Donna's part to adequately achieve academically that which *was* within her capacity. The underlying fear and anxiety with which she viewed academic tasks manifested themselves frequently in such failure. Caroline Jameston now knew, as did Donna in her innermost thoughts, that no amount of academic success or achievement would meet her parents' aspirations.

The dinner that evening was at the country club in which was the finest restaurant in the city. Conversation around the dinner table covered a wide range of topics, carefully avoiding discussion of Donna, until Mrs. Walker, unable to control her anxiety any longer, turned to her husband and said, "Let's ask Donna's teacher about Donna."

"Well, what about her, Miss Jameston," asked Mr. Walker. "Is Donna going to make it, or isn't she? Is she going to snap out of this, or not?"

The topic was now out in the open and Miss Jameston knew that she would have to tread very carefully indeed to avoid either misrepresentation of her program, or the infliction of undue damage to the hopes and aspirations of Mr. and Mrs. Walker. "I'm not sure that I understand just what you mean by 'make it' or 'snap out of it,' " said Miss Jameston softly.

Mr. Walker colored slightly. "Well, what I mean is, are you going to be able to get her back up to grade level, you know, where she should be, so that we can get her into college?"

"John, I don't think . . ." began Mrs. Walker.

"No, I think we have to get this out once and for all," said Mr. Walker. "What about it, Miss Jameston, how does it look to you?"

Gently, but firmly, Caroline Jameston explained that the special class for retarded children was not a remedial class. It was not designed, she continued, to bring children up to grade level. Donna was working up to grade level for her particular capacity; she would improve, but the improvement would be slow, and at best she could be expected to attain sixth grade academic achievement. While Donna was beyond all the children in Miss Jameston's class in terms of her social competency and skills, nevertheless it was extremely unlikely, she pointed out, that Donna would be able to handle the work in an academic high school, much less enter college. The special class would take her as far as she could go, academically, while at the same time attempt to prepare her for the world of work rather than the world of higher education.

"What do you mean, 'the world of work'?" insisted Mr. Walker. "You mean become a servant or a housemaid? Not my daughter. I won't . . ."

"John," interrupted Mrs. Walker, laying her hand gently on her husband's sleeve, "Miss Jameston is only explaining to us what we already know."

Both parents listened quietly as Miss Jameston described Donna's strengths and weaknesses and the role of the special class. "There is much that Donna will be able to do," she continued, "particularly if we can begin to put the major emphasis on her strengths rather than emphasize her academic weaknesses."

Mrs. Walker leaned forward. "Tell us how, Miss Jameston. We'll try."

It had been a long day. The lights of her automobile cut through the darkness as she drove slowly and reflectively home. In the lives of two very different children she had undertaken to bring about some change. This was only the beginning, and there would be many other visits and conferences. Fully as important as any hours she might spend with the children in the classroom had been these attempts to understand the home environment of her children. Armed with the information gathered, she could more fully understand the behavior of her children and plan a more realistic program for them.

Tomorrow was another day.

The lights in the school building burned brightly the following Wednesday evening, and the voices of the parents assembled in the auditorium echoed loudly through the remainder of the deserted building. It was the first Wednesday since the opening of school and a special meeting had been called of the Parents and Teachers Association of the classes of the mentally retarded in the city of Credo. Most of the parents assembled in the auditorium had assumed a dual responsibility; while many were active in the regular Parents and Teachers Association, they had undertaken to form this special association of parents and teachers of retarded children to resolve their special problems.

The size of the group never failed to impress Caroline Jameston. Impressive also was the vitality of the group and their concern for the development of a dynamic, professionally sound educational program for their retarded children. Many of these parents had had personal experience with years of lack of service on the part of the public schools for their retarded children. The special education classes which existed in the city of Credo were due largely to the efforts of these organized parents. They did not perceive their task as completed but rather viewed the establishment of special classes for the retarded as the first step in the development of a special education program of which they could be truly proud.

As Miss Jameston looked about the auditorium she noted several of the parents of children in her class and she moved about through the clusters of people to be sure that she personally visited with each of these. She noted with some pride that the principal of her school was present at this meeting. His presence reflected his growing interest in the program for the mentally retarded in his school.

At 8 P.M. Mr. Mistle beat the gavel on the table and called the meeting to order. After going through the preliminaries, he turned the meeting over to Mr. Black, the Director of Special Education for the city of Credo, who welcomed the group to their first meeting. He described the growth in the program during the past year and the procedures which had been undertaken to solve the transportation problems. He spent some time discussing with them the development of the work-school program in the secondary school, and asked the assembled parents to get busy and work with the civic organizations in developing work opportunities in the community for the retarded adolescents who were trainees in the work-school program.

The growth of this newly instituted endeavor to bridge the gap between school and the world of work, as well as the growth of the total education program for the mentally retarded was, he pointed out, contingent upon the degree of understanding and acceptance developed in the minds of the citizens of the city of Credo. Mr. Black reminded the group of the need to attract to membership persons who were neither parents nor teachers of retarded children, but who were simply interested in this broad social problem. The attraction of such persons would be one aspect of the kind of community education so necessary for the successful development of programs for the retarded, and for the development of job opportunities for the graduates of the special education program. He pointed out that unless this were done the graduates of these special classes were likely to encounter prejudice and misunderstanding when they attempted to find employment. A major problem which Mr. Black presented to the group related to the need to attract to the program for the retarded creative young people interested in a professional career as teachers of the mentally retarded. He pointed out with pride that last year they had had no turnover of teachers in the program for the retarded in Credo, and that the development of new special classes was not impeded by lack of qualified teachers. However, other communities within the state had encountered extreme difficulty in their attempt to secure qualified teachers. He pointed out that the lack of trained teachers in the field of education of the mentally retarded was tantamount to a national educational crisis. Credo was indeed fortunate to have a program of such quality and a Board of Education that had the wisdom to establish personnel policies and salary schedules that made development of this type of program possible.

He concluded: "Ladies and Gentlemen, I have noted a number of aspects of our community's program for the retarded to which we may point with pride. I have also noted areas needing further effort on our part.

"It seems to me that the enterprise in which we are engaged has implications going far beyond the meeting of the practical needs of the retarded in Credo. Rather, our efforts reflect and contribute to changing concepts of the responsibility of our educational system and the goals of education. The provision of free common schools for all was at one time considered to be all that was necessary in order to implement democracy in education. We here, in our efforts on behalf of the retarded, have gone a step further. We hold that only when *special* programs are available to meet the special needs of some of our children can we claim to be truly democratic in our educational philosophy and practice. Our efforts to meet the special needs of the retarded place us in a leadership position in reference to implementing democracy in education throughout our nation's schools. There is no common educational program into which we strive to force children—rather, there must be many programs designed to enable each child to achieve his own unique potential. Ladies and Gentlemen, thank you for inviting me to your meeting."

Mr. Mistle thanked Mr. Black for his presentation and opened the meeting to new business.

"Mr. Chairman." The heads of the members of the audience turned as the voice from the rear of the room echoed throughout the auditorium. With a start Miss Jameston realized that Mr. and Mrs. Walker had been in the audience and that the voice had been that of Mr. Walker, who had risen to his feet to address the chair. This was the first time that Mr. and Mrs. Walker had attended a meeting of the Association, and Caroline Jameston knew that such attendance represented a gigantic step in the direction of overcoming their reluctance to accept Donna's retardation.

"Mr. Chairman," said Mr. Walker again, addressing now both the audience and the chair. "It seems to me that there is a very definite need for some guidance in reference to future growth of our organization."

Caroline Jameston felt tears start to her eyes. She knew that in the brief space of an hour Mr. Walker had been engaged in a struggle, a struggle between his professional skills as a person accustomed to leadership in community endeavors, and his reluctance to identify himself as the parent of a retarded child. The professional man had won.

"There are, I am sure, throughout the United States, dozens, if not hundreds of organizations similar to ours. We have just heard of some of the problems which other communities face in their endeavors to develop a program for their retarded children. I am sure, on the other hand, that there must be some communities which have already resolved the problem of community education and the establishment of job opportunities for their retarded children—problems which we are now facing. Is it not possible that the time has arrived to consider affiliation with a national organization so that our endeavors will be part of a broader, national movement and so that we might benefit from experience of others, and lend our experience to those less fortunate? Some of you assembled here are aware of my position as a lawyer in this community. I would like to advise you that during the course of my professional activities I have had occasion to read a report on *Law and the Mentally Retarded,* prepared by the President's Panel on Mental Retardation. One of the authors of this document is a representative of an organization called the National Association for Retarded Children. Would it not be in order for an organization to secure additional information regarding the National Association for Retarded Children, and to undertake to consider the issue of affiliation with such a national association?"

Mr. Walker sat down. His face was flushed and his hands trembled a bit in a manner quite unfamiliar to a person so accustomed to addressing juries, community organizations, and professional groups. Miss Jameston knew that the trembling of Mr. Walker's hands was not a reflection of any tension he felt when called upon to address people. Rather, it was the result of the giant step he had taken—the step of identifying himself as the parent of a retarded child, and undertaking to participate with others who had so identified themselves.

Mr. Mistle said, "Thank you, sir. And that brings us to the report of our committee that was appointed last year to investigate association with the National Association for Retarded Children. I would like to thank you for your contribution, Mr. Walker, and to express our delight in having you in the audience this evening. If we should decide to become a member unit of the National Association, perhaps you would be willing to help us with the drafting of the constitution. We could use the help of a good lawyer in this organization. Mrs. Hutt, could we have the report of the committee to investigate affiliation at this time?"

Mrs. Hutt rose and walked to the microphone at the front of the room and began her prepared presentation. "The National Association for Retarded Children is a parent-sponsored voluntary health association. I have here the requirements for membership. The constitution of a newly applying local unit must contain the words "retarded children" in the name. The purposes must not be in conflict with the National Association. The primary objective shall be the welfare of *all* mentally retarded persons. Membership is open to parents and friends of mentally retarded persons living in the area around the unit. The benefits of joining are: (1) that we will be part of a national movement to help all retarded children; (2) that we will have access to consultant services regarding vocational rehabilitation, education, public health service, institutions, fund raising and public information; (3) you will each receive a bimonthly publication *Children Limited* which contains up-to-date information on what is going on in the field, and a feature on one of the areas of programming; (4) you will have an opportunity to participate in the annual convention of the organization; and finally (5) 85 percent of all the funds we raise remains in our community. Respectfully submitted, Mrs. John Hutt, Chairman, Committee to Investigate Affiliation with the National Association for Retarded Children. I move that the report be accepted."

The motion was seconded and accepted. As soon as the motion had passed, several people jumped to their feet. "I don't like it," said Mrs. Saunders. "I don't like it one bit. Why do we have to call ourselves 'retarded something or other'? Why can't we call ourselves 'exceptional children's association' or just 'PTA'?"

Mrs. Hutt responded by saying, "Well, this organization is for the mentally retarded. They support and assist and work with other organizations but their identity is with this particular group of children, so they maintain the identity in their name."

The opinions varied and the discussion became quite heated, until finally Mr. Walker was recognized. Again, in the manner of a man who knows precisely what his goals are and has a clear picture of the path to that goal, Mr. Walker addressed the assembled parents and teachers.

"Look," he said, "it took me a long hard time to reach the point where I can admit to myself and to others that my child is not the victim of poor teaching, nor is she going to 'snap out of it,' nor is she going to go to college. My child is mentally retarded. I can understand the feelings of some of you, understand them very well, because I have had them myself. As a matter of fact, it is precisely those reasons that have kept me away from your meetings; it is precisely those feelings that I have brought with me to this meeting this evening. Ladies and Gentlemen, it is a pleasure for me to get rid of those feelings and to feel the strength to be able to admit to myself and to you what I have known for a long, long time. Here we are talking about getting the general public to accept our retarded children, and I am afraid that some of us are just not willing to accept it ourselves. The time has come for us to get rid of those feelings; the time has come for us to stop contributing to the general public's misconceptions about retarded children. The time has come for us to join with the National Association and to get on with the work that confronts this entire nation. Mr. Chairman, I would gladly work with the committee to develop the constitution needed for us to affiliate ourselves with the National Association for Retarded Children. Mr. Chairman, I move that this group affiliate itself with the National Association for Retarded Children."

The applause which rocked the auditorium was spontaneous and prolonged.

Alone, in the quiet of her apartment that evening, Miss Jameston reflected upon the personal and social drama that she had witnessed earlier.

CHAPTER 4

The Profession

The convention hall resounded to the voices of the 3,000 teachers, administrators, and college professors assembled. From the length and breadth of the United States and Canada, persons interested in the welfare of all exceptional children were assembled for the week-long national convention of the Council for Exceptional Children.[1]

Caroline Jameston looked over her program, scanning the lists of panels, film showings, and symposia dealing with the educational and psychological problems of the visually handicapped, the speech and hearing handicapped, physically and emotionally handicapped, the mentally gifted, and the mentally retarded. Her primary inter-

[1] The Council for Exceptional Children, a department of the National Education Association, is an organization whose main function is to improve educational opportunities for exceptional children. It contributes significantly to the professional background of persons who work with them and helps to coordinate various activities for the advancement of the cause.

The CEC is interested in all children who, because of some deviation from the normal, require special educational opportunities.

est lay, of course, in the panels and presentations dealing with the problems of the mentally retarded. However, she knew that the work on behalf of the mentally retarded was an aspect of the broader problem of meeting the needs of all deviant children regardless of the nature of their exceptionality.

It had been an exciting week. Caroline Jameston had learned a great deal from the papers presented in the workshops, and also through the exchange of ideas with the special education teachers from all over the United States. She had many opportunities during this convention week to learn of new types of programs and of new techniques and procedures for solving the various problems within the classroom. In addition, she had broadened her circle of acquaintances and had in the course of the convention become fast friends of two teachers from Canada. They had arranged for the mutual sharing of information, and had talked at great length of spending their vacation together in Montreal. At the reception held in the hotel for teachers from her state on the previous evening, she became aware of programs which previously had not come to her attention.

The large 10-by-5-foot bulletin board in the main lobby of the hotel had been covered in its entirety with information concerning teaching positions available in the field of mental retardation and special education in general. Interview booths had been established to assist those persons wishing to change their positions. Job opportunities existed throughout the nation. The major problem confronting supervisors and college professors was lack of trained teachers.

In the course of her daily activities as a teacher of the retarded, Miss Jameston had come in contact with several physicians, psychologists and social workers who were also highly interested and involved in the field of mental retardation. She had, through these contacts, become aware of the American Association on Mental Deficiency, an organization of professionals having in common an interest in mental retardation. By attending regional and national conventions of this organization, she had found herself repeatedly stimulated by reports of the work of the nation's top professionals in the fields of medicine, psychology, social work and education. All shared a common interest with her; all were members of a team.

Since the local PTA had joined the National Association for Retarded Children, Caroline Jameston had become a regular recipient of the bimonthly newspaper, *Children Limited,* published by that organization. Through the education columns contained in that publication, Miss Jameston gleaned new ideas and much information. Through the book reviews she had undertaken to expand her professional library, and had on a number of occasions communicated directly with the educational consultant of that organization for assistance in program planning and curriculum development. She had participated in a teachers' workshop co-sponsored by the NARC and the local college. She hoped that during her summer vacation on her way to Montreal it would be possible for her to spend a few days meeting with the consultants in education and vocational rehabilitation at the national office of the Association.

Along with that which was so professionally gratifying, Caroline Jameston was also aware of the factors that contributed occasionally to a sense of professional frustration. Every so often, but less frequently in recent years, Miss Jameston would encounter professional attitudes which deprecated the need for special programs for the mentally retarded and failed to perceive the need for highly trained teachers in this area. The demands of the nation for qualified leadership in all areas sometimes led to a failure to recognize the contribution which the mentally retarded can make to our society. This subtle, and sometimes not so subtle, devaluation manifested itself in a failure to establish special classes where they were needed, in a failure to develop teacher training programs in institutions of higher learning, and in the failure to develop employment opportunities for the mentally retarded. Nor was Caroline Jameston particularly pleased with the salary schedules under which she and her fellow teachers functioned. The fact that the average plumber earned considerably more in the course of the year than did Miss Jameston, and the fact that a secretary without a college degree earned as much as a beginning teacher, contributed to the difficulty in attracting creative and dynamic people to the field of education. On the part of the general public, there existed areas of misunderstanding and prejudice directed at the mentally retarded, and any program concerned with the retarded. These were facts, these defects existed. Yet, as Caroline Jameston surveyed the thousands of professionals assembled at the convention, and as she discussed these defects with her colleagues, she experienced a renewed determination to continue her struggle to overcome these defects in her profession. The many rewards and the ultimate satisfaction were worth the struggle, and the rapid growth of all these organizations reminded her that she had many, many companions in that struggle.

CHAPTER 5

The Organization of Programs

Mental retardation refers to sub-average general intellectual functioning which originates during the developmental period and is associated with impairment in adaptive behavior.[1]

In this definition, adaptive behavior relates to the ability of the individual to comply with the expectations society requires of the average person.

For educational purposes the mentally retarded are divided into the educable, who can learn functional academic skills to approximately the fourth to sixth grade level and are generally capable of economic and social independence if given the proper training; and the trainable, who can learn to communicate, take care of their own basic health needs, and become partially self-supporting with adequate supervision.

In a democratic society, the community and state assume the responsibility for the education of all children. This

[1] Rick Heber, "Modifications in the Manual on Terminology and Classification in Mental Retardation," *American Journal on Mental Deficiency*, Vol. 65, No. 4, 1961.

means that special provisions must be made for those children who cannot benefit sufficiently from the instruction provided in the regular classes.

The aims of the Education Policies Commission [2] have generally been accepted as the goals for special education. These aims are:

1. Self-Realization
2. Human Relationships
3. Economic Efficiency
4. Civil Responsibility

Under the self-realization goals are such objectives as health habits, skills of everyday living (dressing oneself, feeding oneself, personal cleanliness, language development, perceptual training, safety, independent travel, simple number concepts) and some positive skills and attitudes which will allow for proper use of leisure time.

Under the goals of human relationships are included all of the skills which make it possible for us to interact with others in our environment in the process of daily living—communication skills, manners, group activities, etc.

Under the heading of economic efficiency are all of the skills which contribute to the economic usefulness of the individual in the society in which he lives. This begins with the simple little task of following directions; develops to the particular skills that are useful in the everyday activities of the school and home, such as cutting, sorting, tying, stacking, counting and marking; then to the more specifically occupational skills of cleaning up after an activity, putting materials away, knowing where materials are stored, washing things which need to be washed,

[2] Education Policies Commission, *The Purposes of Education in American Democracy*, Washington, D.C., National Education Association, 1938.

PUBLIC SCHOOL ENROLLMENTS OF MENTALLY RETARDED FOR THE 1962-63 SCHOOL YEAR

	Legal Status		Educable		Trainable		% of Total School Enrollment
	Educable	Trainable	No. of Classes	No. Enrolled	No. of Classes	No. Enrolled	
Alabama	P	P	213	3,000	–	–	.37
Alaska	P	P	14	210	–	–	.41
Arizona	P	P	199	2,729	46	561	.93
Arkansas	P	P	84	1,269	–	–	.29
California	M	M	2,500	35,008	336	3,720	1.03
Colorado	P	P	249	4,288	15	140	1.01
Connecticut	M	M	304	3,650	100	1,000	.89
District of Columbia	–	–	–	–	–	–	–
Delaware	P	P	78	1,170	36	355	1.55
Florida	P	P	670	10,050	100	1,000	1.01
Georgia	P	P	341	5,084	5	65	.51
Hawaii	M	M	69	1,104	20	361	.96
Idaho	M	P	90	1,000	2	20	.61
Illinois	P	P	706	10,617	48	475	.54
Indiana	P	P	375	5,692	33	404	.59
Iowa	P	P	365	4,692	56	510	.87
Kansas	P	P	138	1,794	20	180	.39
Kentucky	P	M	150	2,631	21	196	.43
Louisiana	P	P	296	2,300	27	270	.33
Maine	P	P*	60	900	–	–	.42
Maryland	P	P	743	15,798	144	1,556	2.59
Massachusetts	M	M	722	10,517	120	1,251	1.24
Michigan	P	P	279	20,248	29	767	1.17
Minnesota	M	P	530	6,341	49	435	.92
Mississippi	P	P	65	1,014	5	50	.18
Missouri	M	M	1,000	16,000	47	1,100	1.99

Montana	M	P	37	444	2	20	.29
Nebraska	P	P	80	1,127	8	65	.39
Nevada	P	P	72	916	11	118	1.28
New Hampshire	P	P	40	650	2	20	.57
New Jersey	M	M	928	12,096	217	2,700	1.27
New Mexico	P	–	166	1,557	–	–	.65
New York	M	M	1,930	28,972	320	3,218	1.09
North Carolina	P	P	495	8,834	89	1,110	.87
North Dakota	P	–	53	575	–	–	.40
Ohio	P	P**	1,203	18,148	**	**	1.08
Oklahoma	P	P	198	3,278	29	347	.63
Oregon	M	–	184	3,000	5	50	.73
Pennsylvania	M	M	2,369	30,040	303	3,828	1.64
Rhode Island	M	M	104	1,342	29	271	1.13
South Carolina	P	P	231	3,000	20	200	.51
South Dakota	P	P	39	438	18	148	.36
Tennessee	P	P	504	7,900	57	971	1.05
Texas	P	P	1,364	17,444	147	1,597	.87
Utah	M	M	105	1,418	12	148	.61
Vermont	P	–	33	485	–	–	.62
Virginia	P	P	270	4,300	50	500	.52
Washington	P	P	357	5,551	76	1,014	.95
West Virginia	P	P	86	1,114	11	133	.28
Wisconsin	P	P	553	8,295	109	872	1.19
Wyoming	P	P	31	356	3	38	.41
TOTAL FIGURES			21,672	323,886	2,877	31,984	

P = Permissive
M = Mandatory
* = Under the State Department of Mental Health
** = Under the State Department of Mental Hygiene

sweeping the floor, making a bed, clearing the table, washing the dishes, helping prepare meals, preparing vegetables; to the actual functioning on job situations, first directed tasks such as simple chores, to pre-vocational participation; to work in a sheltered workshop or in the community.

To meet these goals for the retarded it is necessary that a total program be developed which will: (1) start early; (2) provide a progressive, developmental program with meaningful activities; and (3) continue over a longer period of time than for normal children and extend into vocational placement and follow-up.

The organization for the educable will include: (1) the pre-school class; (2) the primary class; (3) the intermediate class; (4) the pre-vocational class; and (5) the work–school program.

For the trainable the organization consists of (1) pre-school; (2) primary; (3) intermediate; (4) general secondary; (5) school-workshop; (6) workshop; and for some, (7) sheltered employment outside the sheltered workshop.

The state legal provisions and public school enrollments for the 1962–63 school year are given on the following page. These figures provide an index to the availability of services to the mentally retarded in the public schools.

For the boys and girls in Miss Jameston's class, the special learning needs have been recognized and special learning provisions have been made for their education. And yet, as of this writing, the boys and girls in Miss Jameston's class represent only a minority of the estimated one and one half million mentally retarded children in the United States. At the very best, on a nationwide basis, no more than 25 to 30 percent of these boys and girls are receiving the special education they so desperately need.

For many, immature organisms in an increasingly complex world, the daily demands of the regular public school classes contribute to a mounting sense of insecurity and lack of personal worth. Some of these children, living in communities where special education services are not available, and denied entrance into the regular classes, have no opportunity to develop their potentials and can do nothing other than spend their days at home.

Although the mentally retarded have been with us since the beginning of mankind, it wasn't until the beginning of the nineteenth century that any effort was made to educate this group of individuals. In 1799, Itard did his famous work with Victor, who was known at that time as the savage of Averon. Since 1799 we have moved from one attempt with one individual to the level where, in the United States, we have specialized classes in the local public schools for both educable and trainable level mentally retarded children. There are presently over 320,000 educable mentally retarded enrolled in the public schools in the United States, and over 31,000 trainable level children. In 1922, there were only 22,000 mentally retarded of all levels enrolled in the public schools. The number of class enrollments and that of special classes grows at an increasing rate each year, as we become more aware of the contribution that these people can make to our society, and the serious demands on our manpower to care for them if programs are not provided.

To a very considerable degree the boys and girls in Miss Jameston's class, like the overwhelming majority of the mentally retarded children in the nation, are the products of an increasingly complex society. Because of the intense deprivation which so many of these boys and girls have encountered during their very early years, they approach the school entrance deficient in those skills and understandings which provide a crucial foundation for school success. Their membership in various sub-cultural groups, each having their own peculiar motivational patterns and value systems serves to place these children at odds with the values and requirements of the regular classes in the public schools. As long as our nation was essentially a rural agrarian society, the boys and girls, like those in Miss Jameston's class, did not constitute a particularly pressing problem. When the general level of education for the mass of the population was the fourth or fifth grade, and when it was possible for young men and women to enter occupations in the sheltered atmosphere of rural life, the deficiencies which characterize these children remained largely unnoticed. However, with the concentration of large masses of population in urban areas, with daily living becoming increasingly complex, the requirements of occupations more stringent, and the competition for employment more intense, the social problem of mental retardation has become so pressing that in the words of the late President, John F. Kennedy, "Mental retardation ranks as a major national health, social and economic problem."

While there are over two hundred known causes of mental retardation, these specific disease factors account for only a small percentage of the mentally retarded. In the majority of the mentally retarded, the only thing that appears to be wrong with them is that they have difficulty in learning and that they come from backgrounds marked by intense cultural deprivation. Were you to meet Harvey, Donna, Ralph and Billy in the local supermarket, there would be nothing about their physical appearance to indicate to you that they were mentally retarded. Were you to compare them with a group of children in the regular grades, their intellectual deficiency would become apparent almost immediately. As you noted in the visits to the homes of Ralph and Donna, there appear to be rather important differences between retarded children of the same intellectual level who come from different social economic backgrounds. Although the intellectual level of the children might be the same, the social ability is quite markedly retarded among those who have not had the opportunities to learn the social graces which are so much a part of our modern day society.

To teach these children to deal with the complexities of the world in which they live, to help them rise above the cultural level to which they were born, and to prepare them for marriage, employment, and the raising of a family, is truly a challenge worthy of the efforts of our most creative and able young men and women.

CHAPTER 6

How to Become a Teacher of the Mentally Retarded

The American education system is unique in that there is essentially no federal education system. Each school district is autonomous and each state has its own laws regarding public school attendance, teacher certification, school finances, etc. Thus in order to get an idea of the requirements to be a teacher of the mentally retarded, it is necessary to look at the requirements in the specific state in which one wishes to teach.

This chapter contains a brief description of the state certification requirements in the fifty states and a guide to financial assistance for the student. The Appendix provides a listing of colleges and universities offering an undergraduate sequence of courses in education of the mentally retarded.

STATE CERTIFICATION REQUIREMENTS FOR TEACHERS OF THE MENTALLY RETARDED

ALABAMA

A Class B Education Professional Certificate may be issued to a person who presents credentials showing:

1. That he has graduated with a bachelor's degree from a standard institution and has met requirements as prescribed by the State Board of Education for the training of teachers of special education in one or more areas of exceptionality.
2. That he holds a valid Class B Professional Certificate.
3. That he has earned prescribed credit as listed in the area in which he requests certification.

Mental Retardation:

Subject	*Quarter Hours*	*Semester Hours*
Survey course in education for exceptional children	4½	3
Nature and needs of the mentally retarded, including interpretation of psychological tests	4½	3
Education procedures for the mentally retarded, including materials, methods, and curriculum	4½	3
Electives	9	6

Must include courses, each of which has a credit value of four and one-half quarter hours or three semester hours in at least two of the following areas: arts

	Quarter Hours	*Semester Hours*
and crafts for atypical children, adapted physical education, multiple deviation, language development, and student teaching with the mentally retarded	22½	15

A Class B Special Education Professional Certificate is a conditional permanent certificate which is valid in periods of eight years and is the authority of the holder to teach in areas of exceptionality in which he is certified.

This certificate may be continued for a period of eight years from date of lapse upon submission of proof of successful experience as a teacher for four of the eight years immediately preceding the date of lapse of the certificate, such proof to be in the form of written statements by employers.

This certificate may be continued for a period of eight years from date of lapse upon submission of thirteen and one-half quarter hours or nine semester hours of credit earned in residence at a standard senior college or university approved for the training of teachers within the eight years immediately preceding the date of lapse of the certificate.

If this certificate is allowed to lapse, it may be reinstated for a period of eight years upon submission of thirteen and one-half quarter hours or nine semester hours of credit earned in residence at a standard senior college or university approved for the training of teachers within three years of the date the new certificate is to bear.

Residence credit approved for continuance or reinstatement purposes must be earned in professional education or subject matter areas taught in the elementary or secondary schools.

Class A Special Education Professional Certificate

A Class A Special Education Professional Certificate may be issued to a person who presents credentials showing:

1. That he has graduated with a master's degree from a standard institution and has met requirements as prescribed by the State Board of Education for the training of teachers of special education in one or more areas of exceptionality.
2. That he holds a valid Class B Professional Certificate.
3. That he has earned prescribed credit as listed in the area in which he requests certification.

Mental Retardation:

Subject	*Quarter Hours*	*Semester Hours*
Survey course in education for exceptional children	4½	3
Nature and needs of the mentally retarded, including interpretation of psychological tests	4½	3
Educational procedures for the mentally retarded, including materials, methods, and curriculum	4½	3
Educational procedures for the mentally retarded, including language development and speech problems	4½	3
Internship (The internship is to include student teaching under approved conditions in addition to the required three semester hour or five quarter hour course work section.)	4½	3

	Quarter Hours	*Semester Hours*
Electives	9	6
Must include courses, each of which has a credit value of four and one-half quarter or three semester hours in at least two of the following: arts and crafts for the atypical child, adapted physical education, psychological evaluation of children who are exceptional, language and speech development and associated problems, comprehensive workshops in cerebral palsy, social case work with emphasis upon multiple disabilities and/or cerebral palsy, auditory and visual screening, organization and administration of special education and student teaching	31½	21

A Class A Special Education Professional Certificate is a conditional permanent certificate which is valid in periods of ten years and is the authority of the holder to teach in areas of exceptionality in which he is certified.

This certificate may be continued for a period of ten years from date of lapse upon submission of proof of successful experience as a teacher for five of the ten years immediately preceding the date of lapse of the certificate, such proof to be in the form of written statements by employers.

This certificate may be continued for a period of ten years from date of lapse upon submission of thirteen and one-half quarter hours or nine semester hours of credit earned in residence at a standard senior college or university approved for the training of teachers within the ten years immediately preceding the date of lapse of the certificate.

If this certificate is allowed to lapse, it may be reinstated for a period of ten years upon submission of thirteen and one-half quarter hours or nine semester hours of credit earned in residence at a standard senior college or university approved for the training of teachers within three years of the date the new certificate is to bear.

Residence credit approved for continuance or reinstatement purposes must be earned in professional education or subject matter areas taught in the elementary or secondary schools.

ALASKA

A bachelor's degree with a minimum of eighteen semester hours in professional education (twenty-four semester hours for elementary) including a course in methods of teaching and practice teaching, plus either a major in the area of special education or six semester hours beyond the degree in special education subjects.

ARIZONA–No special requirements.

Certification of teachers of the physically handicapped or the mentally retarded.

1. An Elementary or Secondary Certificate based on a bachelor's degree and eighteen semester hours of education.
2. Fifteen semester hours with a minimum of two semester hours in each area from the following:
   - Education (or psychology) of exceptional children
   - Nature and needs of the physically handicapped or the mentally retarded

Education procedures for teaching the physically handicapped or the mentally retarded
Speech and language development (including speech correction)
Directed teaching *

3. Nine semester hours of electives, in addition to the requirements above, with not more than three semester hours in any one area from the following:
   Nature and needs of the physically handicapped or the mentally retarded
   Educational procedures for teaching the physically handicapped or the mentally retarded
   Speech and language development (including speech correction)
   Psychology (abnormal, or relating to handicapped)
   Guidance (including mental, social or vocational adjustment)
   Intelligence testing
   Arts and crafts
   Child development
   Diagnostic or remedial reading
   Medical or other specialized courses relating to the handicapped

CALIFORNIA

Cal. Administrative Code 391 Definitions. (a) Exceptional Children as used in this article means all physically and mentally handicapped minors as defined in Education Code Sections 6801, 6901, 6902, and 6903. (b) "Acceptable" as used in this article means accepted for credentialing purposes by the California State Board of Education.

* Teachers with two years of experience will not be required to take Directed Teaching.

Cal. Administrative Code 392 Application. An applicant for the credential to teach exceptional children shall comply with the procedure prescribed for application (Section 201) and shall have completed a program including the following minimum requirements:

(a) Possession of a valid regular teaching document of the kindergarten–primary, general elementary, junior high school, or general secondary type, except that an applicant for a credential to teach, in special day classes, exceptional children who are deaf or hard of hearing may substitute for the valid regular teaching document an acceptable bachelor's degree and ten semester hours of acceptable professional work in education required for a regular general teaching credential.

(b) Completion of twenty-four semester hours of upper division or graduate work in an acceptable college or university, including coverage of the following general area and any area of specialization in which authorization is sought.

The *general area* shall include each of the following:

Education of exceptional children
Counseling and guidance for the handicapped
Speech development or speech correction
Four semester hours of directed teaching in the area of specialization. One year of successful full-time teaching experience in the area of specialization may be accepted in lieu of the directed teaching requirement

The *areas of specialization* are in teaching the following exceptional children: visually handicapped, deaf or hard of hearing in special day classes, pupils in remedial classes in speech correction and lip reading, mentally retarded, and orthopedically handicapped including the cerebral palsied. Special preparation required in the respective areas of specialization shall include the following:

Mentally Retarded
- Curriculum and methods of teaching the mentally retarded
- Arts and crafts
- Mental deficiency
- Additional preparation in any area of specialization to complete twenty-four semester hours

COLORADO

Separate certificates for any of the special education fields are no longer issued. It is, however, possible to endorse a valid teacher's certificate to show specialization in one or more of the special education fields.

Applicant for the endorsement, "Special Education–Teaching the Mentally Retarded," must hold a valid teacher's certificate comparable to the new Type A, Teacher Certificate, or one of higher grade.

Applicant must have completed a Colorado State Board of Education approved program of preparation for teaching the mentally retarded as prescribed by an accredited college or university in this state or in another state, together with the recommendation of the institution that the endorsement be affixed to the teacher's certificate held by the applicant. To be approved by the Colorado State Board of Education, a collegiate program in another state for preparing teachers of the mentally retarded may not be of lesser quality than similar programs which have been approved in Colorado institutions. (Colorado State College, Greeley; and University of Denver, Denver.)

CONNECTICUT

I. Hold a bachelor's degree from an approved institution.

II. Be recommended by an institution approved for the preparation of teachers of the mentally handicapped. Such approval involves regional or national accreditation, as well as approval of the State Department of Education in the state in which the institution is located.

III. Have completed general education as follows:

A. *Elementary Level or Grades 1–12.* A minimum of seventy-five semester hours' credit in general education including study in each of the following areas, with at least six hours each in the areas marked with a dagger.

† 1. English
2. Science
3. Mathematics
† 4. Social sciences, including United States history
5. Fine arts

B. *Secondary Level.* A minimum of forty-five semester hours' credit in education including at least three of the following areas in addition to the area of major specialization; areas marked with a dagger require six semester hours each:

† 1. English
2. Science
3. Mathematics
† 4. Social sciences, including United States history
5. Fine arts
6. Foreign languages

7. A minimum of thirty semester hours' credit in one of two fields of concentration appropriate for the particular subject endorsement sought in accordance with the requirements under Secondary Teaching Certificate.
   Note: Because of the limited abilities of mentally handicapped children, previous training for secondary school teaching is considered to have limited appropriateness to this area of education.

IV. Have completed a minimum of thirty semester hours' credit in professional education involving a planned pattern of study and experience appropriate to the level of the special field to be taught and designed to develop understanding of the special field and competency to teach therein. This must include some credit in each of the following areas, and include specific amount of credit where such is specified:

A. *Foundations of Education.* This group includes such areas as: (1) history of education, (2) principles of education, (3) philosophy of education, (4) comparative education, and (5) community sociology, community resources, social anthropology.

B. *Educational Psychology.* This group includes such areas as: (1) psychology of learning, (2) human growth and development, (3) child–adolescent psychology, and (4) mental hygiene.

C. *Curriculum and Methods of Teaching.* This group includes such areas as: (1) methods of teaching, (2) teaching of reading, (3) audio-visual aids in education, (4) individualizing instruction, (5) educational measurements, (6) principles of curriculum construction, (7) the curriculum at a particular level, (8) the curriculum in one special field, and (9) extracurricular activities.

D. *Supervised observation, participation, and full-time responsible student teaching,* which may include clinical practice or laboratory totaling at least six but not more than twelve semester hours' credit. One year of successful experience teaching mentally handicapped children in a public school or an approved private school, as attested in writing by an employer, may be accepted as ground for waiving the inclusion of this phase of the professional preparation.

V. The total program must include, as a part of or in addition to the professional preparation in IV, special preparation for teaching the mentally handicapped aggregating not less than twelve semester hours which will be expected to be distributed as follows:

A. Curriculum planning, methods and materials for teaching mentally handicapped children, four to six semester hours. (Examples of such courses might be: Education of mentally retarded children; Principles of teaching the mentally retarded; Materials for teaching the mentally handicapped; Methods of teaching the mentally retarded.)

B. Nature and Needs of the Mentally Handicapped, three semester hours. (Examples of such courses might be: Problems in mental deficiency; Psychology of the mentally handicapped; Nature and needs of mentally handicapped children.)

C. At least one other course specifically related to the education of Mentally Handicapped Children.

(Examples of such courses might be: Occupational education of the mentally retarded; Guidance of the mentally handicapped; Manual skills for the mentally retarded; Household and industrial arts for the mentally retarded; Shop and occupational activities for the mentally handicapped; Diagnostic and improvement of reading and speech difficulties for the mentally retarded.)

Note: If the twelve-hour semester requirement is not fully met through courses in items A, B, and C above, not more than one additional course will be considered acceptable toward the basic requirement from among such more narrowly or less directly related courses as the following: Art (or music) for exceptional children; Handicrafts; Arts and crafts for elementary teaching; Psychology of exceptional children; Problems in the education of exceptional children; Teaching reading to slow-learning children.

Although no distinction is made in certification requirements between *trainable* mentally handicapped and *educable* mentally handicapped, it should be recognized that preparation for teaching one category does not of itself constitute preparation for teaching the other. Candidates and preparing institutions are urged to include preparation for both types of teaching in the program for certification, and to see that candidates accept positions in which they are prepared to offer effective service.

Persons holding valid Connecticut certificates for teaching elementary grades, kindergarten through eighth or any part thereof, may obtain endorsement for teaching mentally handicapped children by completing that portion of the foregoing requirements related to the special preparation required, including practice teaching with mentally handicapped children. One year of successful experience in such teaching will, of course, be accepted as grounds for waiving the practice teaching requirement, provided such waiver is acceptable to the recommending institution.

It should be borne in mind that the preparing institution may, if it sees fit, require preparation in excess of certification requirements before giving its recommendation.

DELAWARE

Exceptional Children

A. Educable Mentally Retarded (Elementary level)

1. Bachelor's degree
2. Elementary Teaching Certificate
3. Specialized professional preparation

   Minimum of twenty-four semester hour credits included in or in addition to the regular teaching certificate with courses in each of the following areas:

   Exceptional children.

   Measurements and evaluations utilized to determine individual differences.

   Principles of growth, development and behavior of children.

   Abnormal or clinical psychology or mental hygiene.

   Procedures in methods and curriculum for educable mentally retarded.

   Arts and crafts for mentally retarded.

   Speech development and improvement.

   Specialized practicum—Student teaching of educable mentally retarded—six semester hours.

(If three years of successful teaching is accepted in lieu of the student teaching, one year must be in the area of the educable mentally retarded.)

B. Educable Mentally Retarded (Teen-age level)
1. Bachelor's degree
2. Elementary Teaching Certificate

or

Secondary Teaching Certificate with ten semester hour credits in elementary education distributed as follows:

	Sem. hrs.
Reading	2–3
Arithmetic	2–3
Science or social studies	2–3
Art, music, or physical education	2–3

3. Specialized Professional Preparation

Minimum of twenty-one semester hour credits included in or in addition to the regular teaching certificate with courses in each of the following areas:

Exceptional children

Adolescent psychology

Abnormal or clinical psychology or mental hygiene

Procedures in methods and curriculum for educable mentally retarded

Occupational education

Specialized practicum—student teaching of educable mentally retarded—six semester hours. (If three years of successful teaching is accepted in lieu of the student teaching, one year must be in the area of the teen-age educable mentally retarded.)

C. Trainable Mentally Retarded

1. Bachelor's degree with a major in one of the following:

   Kindergarten

   Early childhood education

   Home economics child development

   Or a degree in elementary education including minimum of eight semester hour credits in one of the above areas.

2. Specialized Professional Preparation

   Minimum of twenty-one semester hour credits included in or in addition to the regular teaching certificate with courses in each of the following areas:

   Exceptional children

   Psychology of trainable retarded children

   Abnormal or clinical psychology or mental hygiene

   Methods in teaching trainable retarded

   Arts and crafts for mentally retarded

   Methods in language development

   Specialized practicum—student teaching of trainable retarded children—six semester hours. (If three years of successful teaching is accepted in lieu of the student teaching, one year must be in the area of the trainable mentally retarded.)

3. Minimum of 2–3 semester hour credits in occupational education for teachers of teen-age trainable groups.

FLORIDA

Education for the Exceptional Child (Grades 1–12)

Applicants seeking certification in one or more fields of Exceptional Child Education shall meet the General Education requirements of all teachers and the Professional Education requirements, *except as otherwise stated,* and shall meet the specialization areas as herein listed. Programs of special education as approved by the National Council for Accreditation of Teacher Education are acceptable for certification purposes in the areas listed below:

Intellectual Disabilities

Certification to teach children with intellectual disabilities will be added to a Provisional Graduate or Graduate Certificate, provided the applicant has completed eighteen semester hours of specialized preparation, which must include credit in each of the following:

a. A survey course in the education of exceptional children
b. A survey course in language development and speech disabilities
c. Biological, psychological and social foundations of mental deficiency, including nature and needs of children with intellectual disabilities and interpretation of psychological tests
d. Educational management of children with intellectual disabilities, including curriculum, methods and materials
e. Six semester hours of directed teaching of children with intellectual disabilities (Three years' experience gained in accredited schools, in regular class-

rooms or with exceptional children may be substituted for directed teaching.)

Certification at the Post Graduate or Advanced Post Graduate Rank in Intellectual Disabilities, Motor Disabilities, Hearing Disabilities, Visual Disabilities or Speech and/or Hearing Disabilities may be granted provided:

Rank II: The applicant holds a master's degree, is qualified or holds a Rank III certificate covering one of the above fields of exceptionality, and has completed twelve semester hours in the particular field for which certification is sought beyond that required for certification at the Rank III level.

Rank I: The applicant holds a doctor's degree, is qualified or holds a Post Graduate Certificate covering one of the above fields of exceptionality, and has completed twelve semester hours at the graduate level in the particular field of exceptionality for which certification is sought, beyond that which is required for the Rank II level.

Varying Exceptionalities

Teachers certified in Varying Exceptionalities are eligible to teach children with intellectual disabilities, intellectual superiorities, motor disabilities, severe hearing disabilities, severe personality and social adjustment problems, and visual disabilities. Twenty-four semester hours in specialized preparation are required, which shall include credit in each:

a. A survey course in the education of exceptional children
b. Biological, psychological and social foundations of

mental deficiency *or* motor disabilities, including cerebral palsy in either case

c. Foundations and pathologies of personality and adjustment
d. Language development and speech disabilities
e. Educational management of children with intellectual disabilities, including curriculum, methods and materials
f. Educational management of children with visual disabilities—partial vision and blindness—including methods and materials
g. Six semester hours of directed teaching of children with any of the above exceptionalities (Three years of teaching experience in an accredited school, either in a regular classroom or with exceptional children, may be substituted for this directed teaching.)

Rank II: The applicant holds a master's degree, is qualified for or holds a Rank III certificate covering one of the above areas of exceptionality, and has completed thirty-six semester hours of specialized preparation, of which twelve semester hours must be at the graduate level. Within the thirty-six semester hours the applicant shall have completed:

a. A survey course in exceptional child education
b. A survey course in language development and speech disabilities
c. A course in administration of special education
d. A concentration of not less than twelve semester hours in one of the six sub-areas below and credit in at least four of the other sub-areas
   (1) Children with intellectual disabilities
   (2) Children with intellectual superiorities

(3) Children with motor disabilities
(4) Children with severe hearing disabilities
(5) Children with severe personality and social adjustment problems
(6) Children with visual disabilities

Rank I: The applicant holds a doctor's degree, is certified or is eligible for a Post Graduate Certificate in one of the areas of exceptionality, has completed twelve graduate hours in special education beyond that required for the Post Graduate Certificate.

GEORGIA

Certification Requirements for Teachers of Children Who Are Educable Mentally Retarded

The basic program of study for those preparing to qualify for the Teacher's Professional Four-Year Certificate to teach Children of Retarded Mental Development is a T–4 based on a bachelor's degree including or supplemented by the following requirements:

A. *General Education*–Approximately sixty quarter hours or forty semester hours that include work in the following: English, science, social studies, mathematics, and related subjects

B. *Teaching Field*

1. Approximately twenty-five quarter hours or sixteen semester hours in specialized content courses for elementary teaching that includes work in the following: reading, mathematics, science, social studies, arts and crafts, music, health and physical education
2. Specialized content for teachers of the mentally retarded, approximately twenty-five quarter hours

or sixteen semester hours that include the following:

a. Survey course on exceptional children (or Psychology of exceptional children)
b. Nature of retarded mental development (or Psychology of mental deficiency)
c. Speech correction (Survey course in speech correction or Speech correction for the classroom teacher or Language development)
d. Psychology of adjustment (Mental hygiene or Abnormal psychology)
e. Psychometrics (or Basic course in tests and measurements)

C. *Professional Field*—A total of thirty quarter hours or twenty semester hours of which e. and f. must be included.

a. Foundations of education (or Introduction to education or History of education)
b. Child development (or Human growth and development)
c. Curriculum development
d. Psychology of learning
e. Materials and methods for teaching the mentally retarded
f. Practice teaching in the elementary school (including working with normal and mentally retarded children)

Requirements for adding the field—Teaching Educable Mentally Retarded Children to a certificate in another area

A. *Professional Certification*

1. Professional Certification can be added to a Pro-

fessional Certificate for elementary grades by completing the requirements in the *B and C* areas that have not been completed.

2. Professional Certification can be added to a Professional Certificate for the secondary teaching field by completing the requirements in the *B and C* areas that have not been completed.

B. *Provisional Certification*

1. Provisional Certification can be added to a Professional Certificate for the elementary teaching field by first completing the requirements listed under B, 2a and 2b.
2. Provisional Certification can be added to a Professional Certificate for the secondary teaching and other fields by first completing the ten quarter hours listed under B 1 regarding the courses, the teaching of reading and arithmetic, and under B, 2a and 2b.

C. *General Instructions*

It is understood that the teacher will take a minimum of two courses additional work each year until the requirements in this area of exceptionality have been met. Six years may be allowed to complete full certification.

Students and teachers are requested to have a planned program with the college or university where they are studying.

As courses are completed, transcripts should be submitted to the Certification Section, State Department of Education, Atlanta 3, Georgia, for credit toward certification. An application for Provisional or Professional Certification should be submitted only when all requirements have been completed.

HAWAII

Teachers qualified for teaching the mentally retarded may have "Qualified for Teaching the Mentally Retarded" listed on the face of the Professional Teacher's Certificate provided they meet the following requirements:

1. Twenty-four semester hours of undergraduate or graduate work distributed as follows:
   - A general survey course in the education of exceptional children
   - A basic course in remedial techniques
   - Curriculum development for the mentally retarded
   - Arts and crafts for the mentally retarded
   - Psychology of the exceptional child
   - Psychological tests and measurements
   - Counseling and interview techniques
2. Practice teaching with mentally retarded.
3. One year of successful supervised teaching of mentally retarded may be substituted for the practice teaching.

IDAHO

State does not yet have certification requirements for teachers in the field of special education.

ILLINOIS

A teacher of *educable* mentally handicapped children must possess a valid Illinois teacher's certificate and meet the requirements in education, psychology and the specialized training as follows:

Required Minimum Areas of Training

(Areas of training are not necessarily course titles)

I. General Courses in Education and Psychology
   A. American public education
   B. Child growth and development through adolescence
   C. Principles of mental health
   D. Speech re-education

II. Field of Specialization—Educable Mentally Handicapped

Work to be taken at a college maintaining a program for the preparation of teachers of the mentally handicapped which is recognized by the office of the Superintendent of Public Instruction.

Required Specialized Work (Minimum 16 semester hours)
   A. Survey of education for exceptional children
   B. Characteristics of the mentally handicapped (educational and psychological) including implications for education
   C. Teaching techniques and materials for EMH children including principles of curriculum and classroom organization, work with parents, reporting, record keeping, etc.
   D. Practicum with educable mentally handicapped children
   E. Pupil evaluation including tests and measurements

III. Background Work
   A. Student teaching with normal children or approved equivalent
   B. Handwork and/or art for elementary schools
   C. Physical education for elementary schools

D. Music for elementary schools

E. Electives (2 areas selected from the following)

1) Guidance
2) Audio-visual aids
3) Related courses in sociology, psychology, home economics
4) Health education
5) Vocational rehabilitation
6) Related courses in other fields of special education

A request for evaluation of training as a special teacher should be accompanied by a complete transcript of credits of previous training. Permissive deviations from these requirements are as follows:

I. Any teacher who has a bachelor's degree with a valid Illinois Elementary Certificate (not Provisional) and a minimum of two years' teaching experience at the elementary level shall be fully approved to teach EMH children (between the ages of five and twenty-one years) after completing the courses listed under II (Field of Specialization–Educable Mentally Handicapped).

This preparation may be completed in two *consecutive* summer sessions, or one academic year.

Teachers with the background as stated above are automatically given credit for the course work listed under I (General courses in education and psychology) and III (Background work).

Temporary Approval for EMH teaching shall be granted for one year after the completion of the first summer's work. All of the requirements must be met by the end of the second summer.

II. Any teacher who has a bachelor's degree with a valid Illinois *High School* Certificate (not Provisional) and minimum of two years' teaching experience shall be fully approved to teach EMH children (between the ages of 13 and 21 years only) after completing the courses listed under II (Field of Specialization–Educable Mentally Handicapped), and the following background courses:

One course in reading methods or the teaching of reading.

One course in *elementary school methods* of teaching one of the following:

a. Mathematics
b. Social studies
c. Science
d. Music
e. Arts and/or crafts
f. Physical education

One course in the practical arts such as: home economics, industrial arts, vocational agriculture.

Temporary Approval for EMH teaching (between the ages of thirteen and twenty-one only) shall be granted after the completion of not less than eight semester hours of the specialized training listed in II (Field of Specialization–Educable Mentally Handicapped). The remainder of this specialized training must be completed by the end of the second summer. If, at the end of the second summer the teacher has not also completed all of the background course work listed above, but has completed the specialized training, temporary approval may be extended for an additional year to permit the completion of the remaining courses required for full approval for teaching EMH.

Illinois Teacher Training Centers having approved two-summer session (sequential) training programs are:

Chicago Teachers College
Illinois State Normal University
Southern Illinois University
University of Illinois

A teacher of trainable mentally handicapped children must possess a valid Illinois Teacher's Certificate and meet the requirements in education, psychology and the specialized training as follows:

Required Minimum Areas of Training

(Areas of training are not necessarily course titles.)

I. General Courses in Education and Psychology
  a. American public education
  b. Child growth and development through adolescence
  c. Principles of mental health
  d. Language development

II. Field of Specialization–Trainable Mentally Handicapped

Work to be taken at a college maintaining a program for the preparation of teachers of the mentally handicapped which is recognized by the Office of the Superintendent of Public Instruction.

Required Specialized Work (Minimum 16 semester hours)
  a. Survey of Education of Exceptional Children
  b. Characteristics of the mentally handicapped (edu-

cational and psychological) including implications for training and/or education

c. Teaching techniques for trainable mentally handicapped including principles of curriculum and classroom organization, work with parents, reporting, record keeping, etc.

d. Practicum with trainable mentally handicapped children

e. Pupil evaluation including tests and management applicable to the trainable mentally handicapped

III. Background Work

a. Student teaching with normal children or submission of evidence of successful teaching experiences in an area of education, special education or some other discipline dealing with children which has provided an experimental background for teaching trainable mentally handicapped children

b. Crafts for young children

c. Physical activities for young children

d. Music for young children

e. Electives (two areas selected from the following):

1) Parent–teacher education

2) Health education

3) Community resources

4) Related courses in sociology, psychology, home economics

5) Related courses in other fields of special education

6) Vocational rehabilitation

A request for evaluation of training as a special teacher should be accompanied by a complete official transcript of credits of previous teacher training.

Permissive deviations from these requirements are as follows:

I. Any teacher who has a bachelor's degree with a valid Illinois *Elementary* Certificate (not Provisional) shall be fully approved to teach TMH children (between the ages of five and eighteen) after completing the courses listed under II (Field of Specialization—Trainable Mentally Handicapped). This preparation shall be completed in two *consecutive* summer sessions, or in one academic year.

Teachers with the background as stated above are automatically given credit for the course work listed under I (General Courses in Education and Philosophy) and III (Background Work).

Temporary Approval for teaching TMH will be granted for one year after the completion of the first summer's work. All of the courses must be completed by the end of the second summer.

II. Any teacher who has a bachelor's degree with a valid Illinois *High School* Certificate (not Provisional) shall be fully approved to teach TMH children (between the ages of thirteen and eighteen only) after completing the courses listed under II (Field of Specialization—Trainable Mentally Handicapped).

This preparation shall be completed in two *consecutive* summer sessions, or in one academic year.

Temporary Approval for TMH (between the ages of thirteen and eighteen only) shall be granted for one year after the completion of the first summer's work. All of the courses must be completed by the end of the second summer.

The Illinois Teacher Training Center having approved

two-summer session (sequential) training programs is Illinois State Normal University.

INDIANA

Certification for Teaching Special Education Classes

Rule 44 of the Teacher Training and Licensing Commission was promulgated on March 28, 1962. This rule provides new certification patterns for all teaching areas.

Six basic certificates will be issued to cover the various positions in the public schools of Indiana. These certificates are:

A. The General Elementary School Teacher Certificate
B. The Junior High School Teacher Certificate
C. The Secondary School Teacher Certificate
D. The Nonconventional Vocational Teacher Certificate
E. The School Service Personnel Certificate
F. The School Administrator and Supervisor Certificate

The auxiliary, subject matter or special area of preparation will be endorsed on the appropriate basic certificate.

Endorsement for Teaching Special Education Classes

1. Endorsement for *Teaching Special Education Classes* qualifies the holder to teach special education classes in the area of exceptionality endorsed on the certificate.
2. Areas of endorsment are:
   A. Orthopedic and special health problems
   B. Partially sighted
   C. Blind
   D. Mentally retarded
   E. Emotionally disturbed

F. Deaf

3. The program leading to endorsement for each of the above areas excepting teaching the deaf will consist of a minimum of twenty-four semester hours, including:
   A. A minimum of eight semester hours in the area of exceptionality indicated above for which the certificate is to be issued, including psychological and physiological bases of exceptionality, special class methods and student teaching in a special class
   B. Four semester hours in elementary teaching methods distributed between mathematics and language arts (Elementary school teachers will already have met this requirement.)
   C. Directed electives in the general area of special education

IOWA

Any person who works in the schools in the field of special education must hold appropriate special service certification in order for the program to be approved for reimbursement by the Department of Public Instruction. The requirements for an Elementary-Secondary Professional certificate are four years of approved college preparation and a baccalaureate degree from a recognized institution; however, for those teachers not fully endorsed, the following statement on temporary approval of special class teachers applies.

The following policies shall govern the Division of Special Education approval of special class teachers employed for the first time since the beginning of the 1959–60 fall term. All teachers employed in special classes prior to the fall term 1959–60 are exempt from these policies.

A. *Teachers Holding Bachelor's Degrees:* Such teachers should be required to have (1) a certificate endorsed for teaching at the level of the instruction to be offered; (2) agree to work at the rate of at least six semester hours per year, in an institution approved for such preparation, toward the completion of a program of preparation for teaching in the proper area of specialization (that is, mentally retarded, physically handicapped, emotionally disturbed, etc.).

B. *Teachers with Less than Bachelor's Degree:* Such teachers would be required to have a minimum of (1) sixty semester hours of college training, (2) a certificate endorsed for elementary school teaching, (3) two years' teaching experience at the elementary school level, and (4) six semester hours in special education completed in an institution approved for this purpose, three of which must be taken in a course in the education of the mentally retarded, physically handicapped, emotionally disturbed, or other area which specifically applies. Such teachers will need to agree to work toward the completion of the bachelor's degree and the special endorsement at the minimum rate of six semester hours per year.

Annual approval for such teachers will be made on the basis of their progress toward the bachelor's degree and the completion of the requirements for the special endorsement at the specified rate.

KANSAS

A valid Kansas teaching certificate, preferably elementary. If not an elementary certificate, at least one course in each: 1) child development and 2) language arts methods.

A minimum of 36 weeks of successful service in a full-time paid professional position.

General competencies to be acquired through eight to twelve semester hours of course work prescribed by the recommending teacher education institution. Any one course may be used or counted in acquiring more than one proficiency.

An understanding of exceptional children and the field of special education.

An understanding of the home, school and community relations of exceptional children.

Knowledge and skill in the techniques of counseling and interviewing with special application to working with parents of exceptional children.

An understanding of the role of the special education teacher in the total program of educational, medical, psychological and welfare services in the community and sufficient background to receive and to use confidential information from these sources.

Additional Requirements for Teacher of Severely Handicapped (trainable) Children

At least four semester hours of credit in related background areas, including course work in two of the following: speech correction, psychology of adjustment, human physiology or human biology.

At least twelve semester hours of additional credit, including course work in each of the following fields:

Mental retardation and related research, including clinical types.

Classroom organization for classes for severely retarded children.

Curriculum development, including methods and materials for severely retarded children.

Survey of residential schools and sheltered workshops.

Supervised teaching of severely retarded children, at least a part of which shall be in a state training school.

Tentative Approval

Upon recommendation of the employing superintendent, provisional approval may be granted for one year at a time to a person who holds a Kansas teaching certificate, and who engages in a continuous program of study leading to permanent approval or who participates in an in-service training program prescribed by the Division of Special Education.

KENTUCKY

1. *General Education*

   All types of certificates for teachers of exceptional children shall include the same general education as is included in the program of preparation for elementary and/or secondary teachers. (Each institution submits its program of general education through the Division of Teacher Education and Certification to the State Board of Education for approval.)

2. *Majors or Minors or General Requirements*

   If the student pursues the secondary program of teacher preparation for teaching exceptional children, the same areas, majors, and/or minors may be included as for secondary teachers except that one area or one major or one minor may be in the area of special education.

   If the student follows the elementary program, the same twenty-six hours of general requirements shall be included as for elementary teachers. (See page 55, January, 1962, *Bulletin,* State Department of Education.)

3. *Professional Requirements and/or Specialization*

Each of the following types of certificates may be issued upon the completion of a program according to the Items 1 and 2 and according to the following guidelines in *Professional education* and in the area of specialization:

a. *Mental Retardation (Educable)–Area of Preparation*

Professional Requirements. When a teacher pursues the four-year program for preparation of elementary teachers, a minimum of twelve semester hours in special education in the following areas may be accepted as part of the twenty-four semester hours of required work in professional education:

Survey course in education for exceptional children

Nature and needs of mentally retarded children, including the Interpretation of psychological tests

Educational procedures for the educable mentally retarded children, including Methods, Curriculum and Materials, as well as Language development

A minimum of three semester hours or a maximum of four semester hours in student teaching of educable mentally retarded children may be accepted in partial fulfillment of the eight semester hour requirement in student teaching. (A teacher with two years of experience may take in lieu of the three semester hours professional laboratory experiences.)

When the student is pursuing the secondary program of preparation, a minimum of nine semester hours described above may be used in partial fulfillment of a major or minor. Each college which offers a major or minor in mental retardation will determine the additional courses with which to supplement the required nine semester hours and will submit the total for approval. (Twenty-four semester hours for a major—eighteen semester hours for a minor.)

Area of Specialization. The additional courses may be selected from the following:

Teaching of reading (required for those pursuing the secondary curriculum)
Arts and crafts for the mentally retarded
Abnormal psychology
Mental deficiency
Speech and language development
Guidance and testing

b. *Mental Retardation (Trainable)—Area of Preparation*

The program of preparation-certification of teachers of the trainable mentally retarded shall be the same as the program for the educable mentally retarded except that a course entitled "Educational Procedures for the Trainable Mentally Retarded Children, including Methods, Curriculum and Materials, as well as Language Development" shall replace the course entitled "Educational Procedures for the Educable Mentally Retarded Children, including Methods, Curriculum and Materials, as well as Language Development"; and,

The three or four semester hours in student teaching in special education shall be with the trainable mentally retarded children.

c. *Supervision–Area of Preparation*

The holder of a Special Education Certificate in a specific area of exceptionality may have that certificate endorsed for supervision of Special Education programs upon the following conditions:

Two years of successful experience as a teacher of special education or as a public school speech and hearing therapist.

Completion of an approved curriculum leading to a master's degree.

The professional education courses for the preparation of the supervisor shall include fifteen semester hours covering the three areas of:

a) Organization, supervision and administration of special education programs.
b) Special education class areas other than the area of exceptionality of the special education teaching certificate.
c) Speech and hearing unless the teaching certificate is in the area.

A minimum of one course should be taken in each and with a balance in these three aspects of the program. The remaining curriculum may be selected from the professional education curriculum for general supervision or from general education.

The endorsement shall be on a continuing basis so long as the teaching certificate is valid provided the holder is not inactive as a supervisor for longer than a four-year period. If the holder is inactive for more than four years, requirements current at the time the applicant desires a certificate shall be met.

The completion of the baccalaureate degree shall be

minimum basis for the Provisional * Certificate in Special Education. The completion of the master's degree including a minimum of nine semester hours in professional education and a minimum of twelve semester hours in non-professional courses shall be the minimum for the Standard Certificate in Special Education. (Effective 1961–1962)

The Provisional Certificate in Special Education shall be valid for ten years on a continuing basis provided the certificate is registered at the end of each ten-year period in the Division of Teachers Education and Certification of the State Department of Education on evidence of three years' teaching experience or twelve semester hours' additional graduate work (four semester hours' graduate work for each year the teacher fails to teach). If the holder fails to meet the requirements for life extension before the certificate expires, the certificate may be registered, at the end of each ten-year period, in the Division of Teacher Education and Certification on the basis of four semester hours of graduate work in lieu of each of the three years the holder fails to teach.

A student may pursue the four-year program of preparation for elementary or for secondary teachers as a basis for preparing for certification for teaching exceptional children. The student may qualify for dual certification.

A student completing a four-year program of preparation for secondary or elementary teachers in an institution which does not offer an approved program in special education may plan cooperatively with an institution which has this approval and with the State Department of Educa-

* It is recommended that teaching certificates be endorsed for each area of preparation in special education completed and that the endorsement indicate "Provisional" or "Standard."

tion for completing the segment of preparation in special education in an institution which is approved for offering the program.

An institution which provides a program of preparation for teachers of exceptional children may offer the special education segment of the program as graduate or undergraduate courses.

This program may become effective any time after an institution has submitted its program to the State Board of Education through the Division of Teacher Education and Certification and has received approval. It shall become effective for freshmen entering the program September, 1961.

The Certificate in Special Education shall be a twelve-grade certificate.

The teacher of Home Instruction and/or Hospital Instruction may serve on a regular elementary certificate if the majority of the children are of elementary school age or on a secondary certificate if the majority of the children are of high school age. It is recommended that these teachers qualify for special education certificates.

A teacher who qualified in another state on basis of completion of a four-year program of teacher preparation including a planned and approved program in special education in an accredited college may be issued a comparable certificate in Kentucky under the State Board plan of reciprocity.

A holder of a regular elementary or secondary certificate (if the holder has a degree) may have the regular certificate endorsed for a specific area of special education for one year upon completion of a minimum of nine semester hours selected from the approved program. A minimum of six additional semester hours selected from the required program shall be earned for additional annual endorsement. (The rank will be based on the regular certificate and highest degree held.)

Experience on a special education certificate may be accepted on the renewal and/or life extension of the elementary or secondary certificate.

A teacher or supervisor of special education for exceptional children who was employed prior to April 12, 1952, as a teacher or supervisor of special education may serve on any valid teaching certificate in the area of special education in which he has been employed and/or in which he has had previous education.

LOUISIANA

1. Baccalaureate degree from an accredited institution of higher learning and a valid, regular Louisiana certificate to teach normal children in elementary or secondary schools.
2. General requirements in special education for all teachers of exceptional children (minimum of twelve semester hours):

	Sem. hrs.
* Mental (or Educational or Psychological) tests	2
* Child and/or Adolescent psychology	2
* Psychology of (Introduction to, Education of) exceptional children	2
* Arts and crafts	2

Balance of twelve semester hours, if any, from:

Group psychotherapy, group dynamics, psychology or personality development, social psychology, abnormal psychology, organization and administration of classes

* Required courses

for exceptional children, child and/or vocational guidance, mental hygiene.

For Teachers of the Mentally Retarded (Minimum of six semester hours)

	Sem. hrs.
Psychology and/or education of the mentally retarded	2
Curriculum and methods for the mentally retarded (including observation of teaching of the mentally retarded)	2
Arts and crafts (in addition to the course in 2, above)	2

MAINE

Authorization:

To teach physically handicapped or exceptional children who cannot be adequately taught with safety and benefit in the regular public school classes of normal children or who can attend regular classes beneficially if special services are provided. (Exceptions to these requirements are hospital teachers, speech teachers, and teachers of homebound children.)

Requirements:

Eligibility to this certificate will be established in the following methods:

1. A valid general teaching certificate or a college degree acceptable to the Commissioner of Education.
2. A minimum of six semester credit hours in approved courses related to the areas of specialization, such as:
   Psychology of the mentally handicapped
   Principles of teaching handicapped children
   Child development

Clinical measurements
Mental hygiene
Speech correction
Auditory training
Teaching visually handicapped children

MARYLAND—No certification requirements presently in writing. State Committee currently working on statement.

MASSACHUSETTS

1. A bachelor's degree or a diploma from a four-year course in a normal school approved by the Board of Education.
2. Included in each candidate's program of preparation there shall be a minimum of thirty semester hours in education courses approved for the preparation of teachers of special classes, covering the following areas:
   Industrial arts and/or crafts
   Psychology of subnormal and unadjusted children
   Special class methods
   Educational measurements
   Supervised student observation and teaching

Regularly appointed teachers with three years of classroom experience may qualify on completion of a minimum of twelve semester hours as follows:

	Sem. hrs.
Psychology of subnormal and unadjusted children	2
Special class methods	2
Educational measurements	2
Industrial arts and/or crafts	4
Domestic arts	2

Special class teachers shall be approved by the Department of Education before they assume their duties.

MICHIGAN

Requirements for teachers of exceptional children in the several special education fields are determined by Michigan institutions which obtain approval of the State Board of Education for these programs of teacher education. Persons who have made considerable progress toward meeting these requirements, as previously in force, or applicants from other states who have considerable credit in special education and have obtained temporary approval, will be advised by the Department of Public Instruction in terms of the requirements previously in effect and described below; persons currently enrolled in Michigan institutions or those given temporary approval who do not have more than a minimum amount of credit in special education should consult with the authorities of an institution approved by the State Board of Education for offering the program of their choice.

1. Michigan Life or Provisional-Permanent Certificate with a major in the specific area of special education in which the candidate plans to teach.
2. Bachelor's degree.
3. Four semester hours of directed teaching in the field of special education in which the candidate plans to teach.
4. Twenty-four additional semester hours of credit in course work in special education and related subjects to be distributed as follows:
   a. Required courses .... as indicated below
   b. Specific courses .... as indicated below

c. General and related courses . . . sufficient semester hours to make up the balance of twenty-four semester hours.

Course Work Requirements for Teachers of Exceptional Children

1. Required Courses

	Sem. hrs.
a. Education or Survey of exceptional children	2
b. Mental hygiene	2
c. Arts and crafts (not required of speech correctionists and special subject matter teachers)	4

2. Specific Courses
   The requirement concerning directed teaching in special classes may be waived by the training institution for experienced teachers when approved by the Department of Public Instruction.

Teachers of Mentally Handicapped Children—Eight semester hours required

Mental Deficiency, Problems of Instruction and Methods of Teaching the Mentally Handicapped Child, Problems of Organization and Curriculum in Teaching the Mentally Handicapped Child. Education and Social Control of Mentally Handicapped, or equivalents.

General and Related Courses to be chosen from the following courses:

Mental and exceptional testing
Guidance and occupational information

Speech correction
Mental deficiency
Delinquency
Abnormal psychology
Anatomy
Social psychology
Social psychiatry
Child welfare, or equivalents

Experimental Program for Approval of Teachers in Type B Programs

In order to help determine the most appropriate training requirements for teachers of trainable children, the Michigan Department of Public Instruction is modifying, for the next two years, the regulations concerning the approval of teachers for Type B classes for the mentally handicapped. The basic requirement that Type B teachers have the usual sequence for teachers of the mentally handicapped will continue in effect. However, if local schools desire to experiment in using teachers with unique backgrounds of experience and training (e.g.) individuals who have had training experiences in nursery school education, homemaking education, occupational therapy, group work, and so forth, the basic requirements may be modified as follows:

1. The teacher in a Type B program must possess a valid Michigan teaching certificate.
2. The hiring school district administrator must prepare a statement indicating the *reasons* for selecting the particular person for the Type B program. This should include a summary of the teacher's past academic and professional experience.

3. The teacher must complete at least six semester hours of academic growth in appropriate related areas each year to be eligible to continue in the Type B program. Evidence of the completed hours must be submitted to the Department of Public Instruction.

Under these circumstances the Superintendent of Public Instruction may grant approval to the use of such teachers for a Type B program even though the individual does not completely meet the requirements for approval as a teacher of the mentally handicapped.

MINNESOTA

1. Every teacher who teaches a special class shall be certified for the special class she is teaching.
2. No state aid will be granted for any teaching service by a teacher not certified for the special class work such teacher is undertaking.
3. Certification of special teachers and supervisors shall be cleared through the Division of Teacher Certification, State Department of Education.
4. Requirements for certification for teachers of the mentally retarded. (Excerpt from Code VI-A-2, State of Minnesota, Department of Education.)
   a. The teacher of state-aided classes for handicapped students shall have a certificate based on special preparation taken at a college or university approved by the State Board of Education to give this instruction. The original certificate valid for two years may be granted to an applicant who does not meet the full requirement. The complete requirements must be met for a renewal of the original certificate.

b. The validity of a certificate for special classes based on a minor in the special fields will be valid on the level (elementary or secondary) for which the basic preparation was taken.

c. The specific requirements are stated below:

1. Graduation from a four-year course with a major for teaching the mentally retarded
2. Graduation from a four-year course with a certificate to teach in the elementary or secondary schools and an approved minor in the teaching of mentally retarded
3. (a) The qualifications for a valid teaching certificate for the elementary or secondary schools with a minimum of two years of successful teaching experience
   (b) An approved minor, or its equivalent, in teaching of the mentally retarded evaluated by an approved college or university

NOTE: Under program 3 a provisional certificate may be obtained after eight credits are completed toward an approved minor in the teaching of mentally retarded. This provisional certificate is valid for two years and is *not* renewable. A regular special certificate will be issued only upon the completion of the requirements of the minor (or its equivalent).

MISSISSIPPI

I. *General Education*	Hours *Sem.*	*Qtr.*
English	12	16
Fine arts	3	4
(A course(s) in art or music will meet the requirement)		

	Hours	
	Sem.	*Qtr.*
Personal hygiene	3	4
Science	12	16
6 semester or 8 quarter hours in biological science		
6 semester or 8 quarter hours in physical science		
Mathematics	12	16
Social studies	12	16
6 semester or 8 quarter hours to be in either United States (American history) and/or world history (European history or history of Western civilization) or both.		
6 semester hours or 8 quarter hours to be in one or more of the following subjects: Mississippi history, geography, political science, sociology, economics, philosophy, religion, general psychology, social psychology, world history or American history. (Not more than 6 semester hours or 8 quarter hours in either world or American history may be counted in meeting the social studies requirement in the area of general education.)		
Speech	3	4
Electives (to be chosen from areas listed above)	0	8
TOTAL	57	84

II. *Professional Education Requirements for Special Subjects Certificates*

	Hours Sem.	Hours Qtr.
a. Human growth and development (Child or adolescent psychology)	3	4
b. Educational psychology	3	4
c. Methods (May be in either special subject field or education or both)	6	8
d. Directed teaching (Not less than 3 semester or 4 quarter hours shall be in the field of endorsement	6	8
e. Electives	0	4
TOTAL	18	28

III. *Minimum Requirements by Class*

Class AA

Authorization: To teach exceptional children in grades 1–12 according to endorsement.

Tenure: ten years. Invalid if holder is out of service five consecutive years.

1. Hold or qualify to hold a Class A special subject certificate endorsed to teach exceptional children and a master's degree which includes 15 semester hours or 24 quarter hours of graduate credit in special education in the area for which Class A special subject field certificate is endorsed. (12 semester hours or 16 quarter hours of graduate credit in the subject of desired endorsement will meet this requirement until September 1, 1962.)
2. Hold or qualify to hold a Class A teacher's certificate (elementary, secondary or special subject) and a master's

degree which includes 24 semester hours or 36 quarter hours of graduate credit in special education. Eighteen semester or 28 quarter hours of the 24 semester hours or 36 quarter hours of graduate credit must be in courses specified for each endorsement in special education. The specified courses are listed under Class A certificates in special education.

Class A

Authorization: To teach exceptional children in grades 1–12 according to endorsement.

Tenure: 5 years

1. Bachelor's degree
2. General education listed previously
3. Professional education listed previously. For beginning teachers, a minimum of three semester or four quarter hours in methods and a minimum of three semester or four quarter hours in directed teaching must be in the area of special education in which endorsement is desired.
4. Specialized Education: All applicants for a Class A certificate in special education are required to earn the following credits:

	Hours	
	Sem.	*Qtr.*
a. Psychology of the exceptional child	3	4
b. Speech correction	3	4
c. Additional credit for endorsements:		
(1) Mentally Retarded		
a) Teaching the mentally retarded	3	4
b) Arts and crafts	3	4
c) Electives	6	8

IV. *Requirements for Permits to Teach in the Various Areas of Special Education*

Permits equivalent to the highest class of certificate which a teacher holds will be issued in the areas of Mental Retardation, Physically Handicapped, Partially Sighted, and Hard-of-Hearing, upon completion of six semester or eight quarter hours in special education including a survey course in special education (Psychology of the Exceptional Child, Education of the Exceptional Child, Special Education, Education and/or Psychology course dealing with the exceptional child) and one specified course in each area of desired endorsement.

V. *Some Electives Accepted Toward Certification in Special Education*

1. Mental Hygiene
2. Remedial and diagnostic reading
3. Individual psychological testing
4. Clinical psychology
5. Special education techniques
6. Abnormal psychology
7. Diagnostic and behavior problems
8. Psychology of personality
9. Personality adjustment
10. Phonetics
11. Vocational and occupational guidance for exceptional children
12. Arts and crafts
13. Courses in area of endorsement not included in Professional Education
14. Courses required in areas of special education related to the area in which endorsement is desired

MISSOURI

The following minimum qualifications have been set up as the standard for approval of teachers for classes of children who are retarded: (Educable)

1. A bachelor's degree from an accredited college or university
2. A valid teacher's certificate in elementary or in secondary education, or a combination of these
3. A background of courses which will indicate adequate preparation in the subject matter and techniques of educating the child who is retarded

   This must include twenty-four semester hours in the following:

   a. An introductory course in the education of the exceptional child (required)
   b. A course in the problems in reading, or remedial reading for the mentally retarded (required)
   c. Methods of teaching the mentally retarded (required)
   d. Courses in arts and crafts (five hours required)
   e. Practice teaching in the area of the mentally retarded (required)
   f. A course in mental hygiene
   g. An introductory course in speech correction
   h. A course in educational measurements
   i. A course in child psychology
   j. A course in adolescent psychology, if the teaching is on the secondary level only
   k. A course in guidance and counseling
   l. Practice teaching at the elementary or secondary level in a regular classroom
   m. A course in child growth and development
4. A course in the techniques of teaching in the elemen-

tary school, if the teaching is on the elementary or extended elementary level

A course in the techniques of teaching in the secondary school, if the teaching is on the secondary level

When the teaching is on both the elementary and the secondary levels and the teacher has had a course in the techniques of teaching in the elementary school, the course in techniques of teaching in the secondary school will be waived. If the teacher has had a course in the techniques of teaching in the secondary school, the course in techniques of teaching in the elementary school will be waived.

Standards for Certification for Teachers of Retarded Children (Trainable)

1. A baccalaureate degree with a satisfactory background in general education and a minimum of twenty hours in professional education:

	Sem. hrs.
The Pupil (educational psychology, child growth and development, child psychology, etc.)	4–6
The School (history or philosophy of education, foundations of education, organization and management, etc.)	4–6
Theory and practice (education of children with retarded mental development, Theory (Trainable), education of children with retarded mental development, Practice (Trainable, Curriculum and materials for children with retarded mental development (Trainable), etc.	6–8
Other education courses	2–6

2. A background of courses (minimum 24 hours) which will indicate adequate preparation in the area of the training program—retarded children (** required courses, * required when available)

	Sem. hrs.
**Music for elementary schools	2
**Physical education for elementary schools or elementary plays and games	2
**Speech for the classroom teacher	3
**Arts and crafts	4
**Introduction to exceptional children or Psychology of the exceptional child	2
*Mental retardation	2
*Arts and crafts for the handicapped	2
*Parent counseling	2
*Children's literature	2
General sociology	3
Audio-visual aids	2
Abnormal psychology	2
Mental hygiene or Psychology of personal adjustment	2
Child care	2
Methods of teaching home economics in the elementary and junior high school	2
Fundamentals of guidance	2
Individual intelligence testing	2

3. Teachers who do not meet the directed requirements may be given temporary certification by the Director of Training of Retarded Children or by the Director of Special Education. Re-certification may be achieved on a one-year basis by removing a minimum of six hours of listed deficiencies on or before September 1, of each school year.

MONTANA

As a minimum, a teacher of a special class of educable mentally retarded children must:

1. Be regularly certified as a teacher in Montana, with minimum of a bachelor's degree.
2. Have a minimum of at least two years successful teaching experience.
3. Have a minimum of fifteen quarter hours in special education. Included in these fifteen quarter hours the following courses are recommended:
   - Introductory course in special education
   - Introductory course in the education of the mentally handicapped
   - Supervised practice teaching with the mentally handicapped

   The following supplementary courses are also recommended:
   - Arts and crafts
   - Counseling and guidance
   - Introductory course in psychological testing
   - Introductory course in speech correction
   - Mental hygiene

NEBRASKA

In addition to, or as a part of, legal certification requirements, special education teachers assigned in a qualified program for the educable mentally handicapped must have completed a minimum of twelve semester hours, as follows:

Educational psychology (including emphasis on human development and behavior—6 hours).

Education of the mentally handicapped (including special methods and techniques, practice teaching or practicum).

NEVADA

Special certificates for teaching the exceptional child:
1) Visually Handicapped
2) Emotionally Disturbed
3) Hard-of-Hearing
4) Mentally Retarded
5) Orthopedically Handicapped

An applicant for a special certificate to teach the exceptional child for any of the types listed above shall possess a regular Nevada teaching certificate of the Elementary Professional or High School Professional type. If an applicant does not hold a Nevada certificate, he may substitute an acceptable bachelor's degree and six semester hours of professional work in education. In addition, an applicant shall have completed twelve semester hours of acceptable college or university credit in specialized and related course work in the area for the type requested. An applicant may be allowed credit for full-time experience in teaching the exceptional child in a public school at the rate of four semester hours for each year of experience to be applied to meet credit requirements, limited to eight semester hours.

Renewal requirements for Special Certificates: These certificates are renewable upon presentation to the certification office of three semester hours of credit earned during the life of the certificate or during the last renewal period, with the exception of Driver Education and Training Certificates. Those holding special certificates based on full college graduation must earn three semester hours of credit within a four-year period to gain subsequent renewals.

NEW HAMPSHIRE

The teacher must meet the academic and professional requirements for an elementary or secondary teacher. Must have completed twelve semester hours in the following areas:

Nature and Needs of the Mentally Retarded
Occupational Education for Mentally Retarded
Methods in Teaching the Mentally Retarded
Observation and Supervised Student Teaching of the Mentally Retarded

NEW JERSEY

Authorization: This certificate or endorsement is required for teaching mentally retarded (educable and trainable) children in elementary, secondary and vocational schools.

I. *Requirements for an Endorsement on a Limited or Permanent Teacher's Certificate:*

A minimum of eighteen semester-hour credits in the following areas or their equivalent, in separate or integrated courses. Work in the starred areas is required:

*1. Introduced to education of the handicapped
*2. Psychology of the handicapped
*3. Curriculum and methods for teaching the mentally retarded (trainable and educable)
*4. Arts and crafts
*5. Orientation in psychological tests
6. Reading disabilities
7. Speech correction

8. Electives related to the education of the mentally retarded

II. *Requirements for Limited Certificate:*

A. Successful completion of a college or university program approved by the New Jersey State Board of Education for the preparation of teachers of the mentally retarded (educable and trainable), and the recommendation of the institution.

OR

B. 1. A bachelor's degree based upon a four-year curriculum in an accredited college.

2. A minimum of thirty semester-hour credits in general background courses distributed in at least three of the following fields: English, social studies, science, fine arts, mathematics, and foreign languages. Six semester-hour credits in English and six in social studies will be required.

3. Thirty semester-hour credits in the field of education, including the eighteen specified for the endorsement in I above, and, in addition, work in the following fields of study, including each of the starred areas:

*1. Methods
*2. Principles and practices of education
*3. Educational psychology
*4. Curriculum
5. Electives

4. One-hundred-fifty clock hours of approved student teaching of children who are mentally retarded (educable and trainable), or one year of approved experience in teaching the mentally retarded (educable and trainable).

Provisional Certificate

1. A provisional certificate for teaching the mentally retarded may be issued to a college graduate who presents eighteen hours of credit acceptable toward the certificate, including at least six semester hours in I above (Requirements for an Endorsement on a Limited or Permanent Teacher's Certificate).
2. A provisional certificate may be issued to the graduate of a two or three year normal school program who has had two years of approved teaching experience, when the candidate presents six semester hour credits from among the specialized areas required for the endorsement as listed under I, above (Requirements for Endorsement on a Limited or Permanent Teacher's Certificate).

NEW MEXICO

Regulations for teachers in the Exceptional Children's Program require the individual to have:

1. A New Mexico teaching certificate valid for the level at which the individual is functioning.
2. Eight semester hours of special training distributed over the areas of:
   a. Exceptional children
   b. Social problems of children
   c. Arts and crafts
   d. Child and adolescent psychology and Growth and development

NEW YORK

Validation for teaching state-subsidized classes of mentally retarded children (educable). The validity of a certificate for teaching the common branch subjects issued upon four years of approved preparation shall be extended by the Commissioner of Education to include the teaching of mentally retarded children (educable) upon evidence that the holder thereof has:

1) Completed a program approved for the teaching of mentally retarded children (educable) at an institution or institutions having a program registered and/or approved by the State Education Department for such preparation; or
2) Completed a twelve-semester-hour program of study to include each of the following areas:
   a) Practicum in teaching classes of the mentally retarded
   b) The psychology of the mentally retarded
   c) Mental and educational measurements
   d) Curriculum practices for the mentally retarded
   e) Creative arts for children

Validation for teaching state-subsidized classes of children with severely retarded mental development. The validity of a certificate for teaching early childhood education issued upon four years of approved preparation shall be extended by the Commissioner of Education to include the teaching of state-subsidized classes of children with severely retarded mental development on evidence that the holder thereof has completed twelve semester hours in professional courses approved for teachers of mentally handicapped children.

NORTH CAROLINA

Programs of preparation for a prospective teacher of exceptional children should provide the basic competencies which every teacher of exceptional children must have. The program should also develop competency and understanding in a particular area of special education. Preparation for teaching in the area of special education should include approximately 25 percent of the total undergraduate program of the prospective teacher, developed in accordance with the following guidelines:

Guideline 1: The program should include an introduction to all areas of special education.
Preparation in this area should include a survey of the general field of exceptional children, including:

a. Emphasis upon the special problems in the education of the specific types of handicapped children—mentally retarded, speech and hearing handicapped, visually handicapped, and emotionally disturbed.
b. A recognition of the physical, social, emotional, and learning characteristics of these children.
c. Opportunity to observe institutions and facilities concerned with the education, health and welfare of all types of exceptional children.

Guideline 2: The program should require a depth in study sufficient to assure reasonable competence in the area of concentration.
Preparation for teachers of the mentally retarded should include:

a. Study of the etiology of mental retardation
b. Characteristics of mentally retarded
c. Classification and diagnosis
d. Social control and adjustment of the mentally retarded, including the role of the family, the school, community agencies, and the institutions

e. Basic information about the education of trainable and educable mentally retarded
f. Interpretation of psychological tests
g. Screening and selection of children for class placement
h. Curriculum development, methods and materials and special teaching techniques
i. Problems related to integration of mentally retarded students into general school organization
j. Laboratory experience with mentally retarded students in educational programs

(Approximately 10 percent of the undergraduate program of the prospective teacher of mentally retarded pupils should be devoted to this area.)

NORTH DAKOTA

At present the teacher of the classroom for educable mentally handicapped children is required to have:

1. A valid North Dakota Teaching Certificate
2. Two years of successful teaching in regular classes
3. At least four quarter hours credit in Methods of Teaching Educable Mentally Handicapped Children
4. Personal qualifications important to teaching the mentally handicapped

Basic Credential: The first step in increasing the training required for teachers in this area will be to require the following by September 1, 1965.

1. A valid First Grade Professional North Dakota Teaching Certificate (with training in elementary, junior high or special education) or any valid North Dakota Teaching Certificate and two years of successful teaching experience in the regular grades or in

special education classes for educable mentally handicapped children.

2. Fifteen quarter hours in special education for teachers of educable mentally handicapped children chosen from the following courses. At least one course from each group must be included:

   Group 1: Mental hygiene or Psychology of adjustment or Personality theory

   Group 2: Methods of teaching educable mentally handicapped children (four quarter hours)

   Group 3: Psychology of exceptional children or Education of exceptional children

   Group 4: a.) Student teaching in a class for educable mentally handicapped children or b.) Advanced seminar (for those with previous teaching experience in a class for retarded children) with an opportunity to work directly with a child or children with specific learning disabilities using projects involving materials and methods. A letter of recommendation from the instructor is required under both plans

   Group 5: Arts and crafts in the public school or for retarded children
   - Remedial reading
   - Abnormal psychology
   - Introduction to speech correction
   - Principles and practices of guidance
   - Other allied courses (with permission)

Anyone fulfilling the above requirements for the Basic Credential may apply for it at this time.

Advanced Credential: Those who achieve further proficiency in the field of teaching educable mentally handicapped children through advanced undergraduate or graduate study may apply for the Advanced Credential upon having completed at least fifteen additional quarter hours in the following areas:

Group 1: (4–6 qtr. hours) Individual appraisal
Introduction to clinical psychology
Individual testing
Abnormal psychology

Group 2: (4 qtr. hours) Education of brain-injured children
Children with perceptual defects

Group 3: (4–6 qtr. hours) Manual skills and Analysis of job areas
Occupational education for mentally retarded children
Guidance for the handicapped

Group 4: (3–6 qtr. hours) Additional courses from Group 5 under Basic Credential

It is understood that the person applying for the Advanced Credential shall have completed the requirements for the Basic Credential and shall have completed the requirements for the bachelor's degree and hold a valid first professional teaching certificate for North Dakota. Not enough graduate level work is available in the state at the present time to provide a Master Teacher designation in this area but this may be developed as offerings increase.

OHIO

An applicant for the professional special certificate to teach slow-learning children, who does not qualify for a provisional elementary or secondary teaching certificate, shall submit evidence of a degree from an institution approved to train teachers of slow-learning children including evidence of the following preparation:

	Sem. hrs.
(1) Child growth and development	2
(2) Psychology or education of exceptional children	2
(3) Education or psychology of slow-learning children	2
(4) Principles and practices in curriculum planning and program development including one course in language arts (including reading), arithmetic, and social studies for slow-learning children	6
(5) Preparation, selection and adaption of instructional materials for slow-learners	2
(6) Occupational orientation and job training	2
(7) Observation and student teaching, at least half of which shall be in classes for slow-learning children	8

An applicant for the provisional special certificate to teach slow-learning children, who holds an elementary or secondary certificate, shall submit evidence of the following preparation:

	Sem. hrs.
(1) Psychology or education of exceptional children	2

	Sem. hrs.
(2) Education or psychology of slow-learning children	2
(3) Principles and practices in curriculum planning and program development including one course in language arts (including reading), arithmetic and social studies for slow-learning children	6
(4) Occupational orientation and job training	2
(5) Observation and student teaching in classes for slow-learning children *	6

OKLAHOMA

1. All general requirements
2. A bachelor's degree from an institution approved for teacher education based upon the completion of a program approved by the State Board of Education for the education of teachers of physically handicapped and slow-learning children in the elementary and secondary schools, including:
   a. A minimum of fifty semester hours in general education designed to develop a broad cultural background with work in at least six of the following: (1) English (oral English, written English and literature), (2) social studies (applicant may satisfy the general requirement in American history and government and Oklahoma history as a part of his required general education), (3) health and physical education, (4) science, (5) mathematics, (6) psychology, (7) foreign language, (8) fine arts and (9) practical arts
   b. A minimum of twenty-one semester hours in profes-

* May be waived upon the completion of eighteen months of successful teaching experience in classes for slow-learning children.

sional education, including at least nine semester hours in student teaching, methods and materials

c. A minimum of twenty-four semester hours of college credit in Special Education subjects

Requirements for the Provisional Teaching Certificate

1. All general requirements
2. One hundred and eighteen semester hours of college credit certified by an approved four-year college or university, including:
   a. A minimum of forty semester hours of credit in general education designed to develop a broad cultural background
   b. A minimum of twelve semester hours of credit in professional education, including student teaching, methods, and materials
   c. A minimum of eight semester hours of college credit in Special Education subjects

OREGON

This certificate is required of all teachers in the state-reimbursed classes for mentally retarded children.

A. Hold, or be eligible for a regular, general Oregon teacher's certificate, either elementary or secondary

B. One year of successful teaching experience in the regular public school classroom

C. Eighteen quarter hours of preparation in special education taken in a standard college or university, this preparation to be distributed as follows:
   1. Education of mentally retarded children—three quarter hours
   2. Curriculum and methods for teaching mentally retarded children—three quarter hours

3. Arts and crafts for mentally retarded children—three quarter hours
4. Supervised teaching of mentally retarded children—three quarter hours (Official evidence of one year of successful experience in teaching mentally retarded children in the public school may be substituted for the supervised teaching requirement. The acceptance of experience does not constitute the granting of any credit.)
5. Six quarter hours of preparation from the following fields:
   a. Speech correction
   b. Diagnostic techniques
   c. Mental testing
   d. Related courses in education of the mentally retarded

PENNSYLVANIA

Effective Currently

I. *Regulations Governing Certificates Previously Issued*
   All Temporary, Special, Normal and Provisional College certificates now valid will be renewed and made permanent in accordance with the conditions on which they were issued.

II. *Regulations Governing the Issue of New Certificates*
   A. A certificate of standard grade valid for teaching the elementary subjects may be extended to include the teaching of classes for the mentally retarded on the completion of twenty-four semester hours of approved courses in special education in accordance with the following suggested distribution:

	Sem. hrs.
1. Courses Basic to All Special Class Certification	6
*Psychology or education of exceptional children	
Diagnostic testing and remedial reading	
Mental or educational hygiene	
2. Courses Definitely Applicable to the Teaching of Mentally Retarded Children	9
*Special class arts and crafts (six semester hours)	
*Student teaching in classes for mentally retarded children (one semester hour)	
*Special class methods	
3. Special Class Electives	9
Clinical psychology	
Abnormal psychology	
**Mental tests (group)	
Speech correction	
Mental tests (individual)	
Corrective physical education	
Educational and vocational guidance	
Related courses in sociology	
***Teaching experience	

Any excess in groups one or two may be applied in group three. A college certificate valid for the secondary field may be extended to include the teaching of classes for the mentally retarded on the completion of thirty-six semester hours, including the distribution in groups one, two and three, in Section A and twelve semester hours selected from group four, below.

4. Courses Related to Elementary Education which Are Basic Prerequisites for Teaching Special Classes for the Mentally Retarded Selected from the Following or Equivalent Courses: 12
   **Teaching of reading
   **Teaching of arithmetic
   Art in the elementary school
   Music in the elementary school
   Health or physical education in the elementary school
   Education measurements
   Principles of elementary education
   Child psychology
   **Elementary school methods
   **Elementary school curriculum
   Teaching of elementary social studies
   Children's literature and storytelling

In institutions approved for the education of teachers of special classes for the mentally retarded, students pursuing the four-year elementary curriculum may elect the above courses in groups one, two, and three, and on the satisfactory completion of the elementary curriculum and the twenty-four semester hours in this special field will receive certification in both fields. Such dual certification will require at least one additional summer session.

* Must be selected within these groups.

** Preferred elective.

***Successful experience in teaching, in social service such as visiting teacher, probation officer, or social worker; in public health work such as school nurse, public health nurse, etc., or in a psycho-educational or psychiatric clinic as psychological examiner or psychologist; may be counted to a maximum of six semester hours at the rate of three semester hours a year.

Effective October, 1963

Certification in Special Education—Elementary—Mentally Retarded (Educable and Trainable).

A certificate valid for teaching in the elementary schools may be extended for teaching exceptional children as follows:

Provisional

Six semester hours of courses in the area of the psychology of exceptional children. Six semester hours of specialized preparation in curriculum and methodology for mentally retarded children including arts and crafts, music and audio-visual aids.

Student teaching experience or observation in classes for mentally retarded children and clinical observation shall be a part of the practice teaching requirement. Teachers fully certified in elementary education in which student teaching has been required may fulfill this requirement with one year of teaching experience in classes for the mentally retarded.

Permanent

This certificate may be made permanent upon the completion of six additional semester hours in psychology related to exceptional children and six additional hours in methodology, curriculum and materials of instruction, and three years of satisfactory teaching experience.

Certification in Special Education—Secondary—Mentally Retarded (Educable and Trainable)

A certificate valid for teaching in the secondary schools may be extended for teaching exceptional children as follows:

Provisional

Six semester hours of courses in the area of the psychology of exceptional children. A basic course in the teaching of reading. A basic course in the teaching of arithmetic. Six *additional* semester hours of specialized preparation in curriculum and methodology for mentally retarded including arts and crafts, music, and audio-visual aids.

Student teaching experience or observation shall be a part of the practice teaching requirement. Teachers fully certified in secondary education in which student teaching has been required may fulfill this requirement with one year of teaching experience in a class for the mentally retarded.

Permanent

This certificate may be made permanent upon the completion of six additional semester hours in courses in psychology related to exceptional children and six additional semester hours in methodology, curriculum and materials of instruction and three years of satisfactory teaching experience.

RHODE ISLAND

Requirements for a Certificate to Teach Classes of Mentally Retarded Children (Educable).

This certificate is valid for teaching classes of mentally retarded children (educable) established under rules and regulations of the State Board of Education.

I. *Provisional Certificate*—valid for three years.
   A. Bachelor's degree from an institution approved by the State Board of Education
   B. Eligibility for a Rhode Island Teacher's Certificate

C. Twenty-four semester hours of courses in the following areas:
Child growth and development
Mental hygiene or personality adjustment
Characteristics and needs of retarded children
Curriculum for retarded children
Theory and methods for retarded children
Manual skills and job analysis
Psychology of education of exceptional children
Practice teaching

Note: The practice teaching requirement may be waived for applicants who have had one year of satisfactory teaching experience with a class of mentally retarded children (educable).

Note: Applicants who have not fulfilled the requirement in Rhode Island Education will be allowed three years in which to meet this requirement.

II. *Professional Certificate*—valid for five years.
A. Same as I-A
B. Same as I-B
C. Same as I-C
D. Three years' successful teaching experience in classes for mentally retarded children (educable) in Rhode Island

III. *Life Professional Certificate*—valid for life.
A. Master's degree (or its equivalent) from an institution approved by the State Board of Education
B. Same as I-B
C. Same as I-C
D. Ten years' successful teaching experience in classes for mentally retarded children (educable) in Rhode Island after receiving professional certification

Requirements for a Certificate to Teach Classes of Mentally Retarded Children (Trainable).

This certificate is valid for teaching classes of mentally retarded children (trainable) established under rules and regulations of the State Board of Education.

I. *Provisional Certificate*—valid three years.
   A. Bachelor's degree from an institution approved by the State Board of Education
   B. Eligibility for a Rhode Island Teacher's Certificate
   C. Fifteen semester hours of courses in the following areas:
      Child Growth and Development
      Mental Hygiene and Personality Adjustment
      Characteristics and Needs of Retarded Children
      Curriculum for Retarded Children
      Theory and Methods for Severely Retarded Children

II. *Professional Certificate*—valid for five years.
   A. Same as I-A
   B. Same as I-B
   C. Same as I-C
   D. Three years' successful teaching experience in classes for mentally retarded children (trainable) in Rhode Island

III. *Life Professional Certificate*—valid for life.
   A. Master's degree (or its equivalent) from an institution approved by the State Board of Education
   B. Same as I-B
   C. Same as I-C
   D. Ten years' successful teaching experience in classes for mentally retarded children (trainable)

in Rhode Island after receiving professional certification

SOUTH CAROLINA

General Requirements

A. Valid elementary teacher's certificate
B. Courses in the areas described below:

	Sem. hrs.
1. Child growth and development and/or methods and materials of teaching the basic subjects in the elementary school	6
2. Introduction to exceptional child education	3
3. Speech correction for the classroom teacher	3
4. Arts and crafts for the elementary school child	3

Special Requirements for Certificate to Teach Mentally Retarded

A total of not less than fifteen semester hours must be earned in courses described in items 2, 3, 4, 5, and 6.

	Sem. hrs.
5. Nature of mental retardation	3
6. Methods and materials for teaching the mentally retarded	3

SOUTH DAKOTA

Possession of a valid degree certificate of the kindergarten, primary, general elementary, junior high school, or general secondary type.

Completion of a total of thirty-six quarter hours of professional training and selected from the following at graduate and undergraduate level.*

* Equivalent semester hours may be substituted.

(a) Three quarter hours' * introduction to problems of exceptional children (psychology of exceptional children)
(b) Nine quarter hours required and selected from:
1. Child development or child psychology
2. Child guidance
3. Mental hygiene
4. Behavior disorders of children (abnormal psychology)
5. Principles and procedures of guidance
(c) Nine quarter hours required and selected from:
1. Methods of teaching or curriculum development for the mentally retarded *
2. Directed student teaching with mentally retarded *
3. Methods or curriculum development for teaching the physically handicapped
4. Directed student teaching with the physically handicapped
5. Orientation to the rehabilitation of physically handicapped
6. Rehabilitation of the mentally retarded and physically handicapped (advanced work)
(d) Fifteen quarter hours required and selected from:
1. Methods of instruction for those with reading problems (remedial reading)
2. Clinical practice in remedial reading
3. Supervision of remedial reading programs
4. Arts and crafts
5. Introduction to speech pathology and audiology
6. Practical application of basic psychological testing
7. Supervision of special education

* Basic requirements for certification.

8. Theory in teaching gifted children (psychology of gifted children)

Tentative Approval

Tentative approval for one school year will be granted to persons who do not hold a degree certificate but have completed at least two years of college work and completed at least nine quarter hours of required course work as follows:

	Quarter hours
Introduction to problems of exceptional children (Psychology of exceptional children)	3
Methods or curriculum development for teaching mentally retarded children	3
Directed student teaching with mentally retarded	3

In addition a person must:

a. Plan a program of study leading to permanent approval (see training standards).
b. Be specifically recommended by an accredited teacher-training institution.

Approval may be extended for one year at a time for five years provided the applicant:

a. Continues to progress according to a plan agreed upon by the applicant and the Division of Pupil Personnel Services. (Some leeway as to consecutive summer preparation will be permitted if just cause can be shown.)
b. Has demonstrated success as a special class teacher.

It is recommended that a person holding a state certificate, and prior to completion of the bachelor's degree (B.A. or B.S.) have, in addition to the nine quarter hours listed above, the following course work:

Six quarter hours of work selected from the following: educational psychology, child psychology, adolescent psychology.

Nine quarter hours of work selected from the following: speech correction, arts and crafts, methods of curriculum development for teaching the physically handicapped, mental hygiene, supervised teaching with the physically handicapped, orientation to problems of the physically handicapped.

TENNESSEE

An applicant for endorsement in educable mentally retarded shall have completed a minimum of sixty quarter hours in the General Education Core plus thirty-six hours of Professional Education, including at least three quarter hours of supervised student teaching in the regular grades and three quarter hours in educational measurement and evaluation. Not less than nine quarter hours and not more than fifteen quarter hours in Psychological Foundations of Education shall be included. The applicant shall have completed at least twenty-one hours in the following specialized preparation:

1. Survey course in exceptional children (required)
2. Specialized course work in mental retardation
   a. Nature and needs of mentally retarded, including interpretation of psychological tests (required)
   b. Educational procedures for educable mentally retarded, including curriculum, methods, and materials (required)
   c. Speech and language development
   d. Teaching of reading and/or remedial reading
3. One of the following required:

a. Supervised student teaching of mentally retarded children
b. A statement from the teacher education institution indicating the applicant has obtained ninety clock hours of practicum with mentally retarded children
c. A statement from the school administration that the applicant has completed two years or more of successful specialized class teaching experience with educable mentally retarded

(Those who began their preparation prior to May 11, 1962, may follow previous regulations.)

TEXAS

Required of All Teachers

Completion of a baccalaureate degree (including six semester hours in American history and the course(s) in Texas and Federal Constitutions).

Completion of a general education program of around forty-five semester hours in courses that provide common backgrounds and foundations of our social and cultural heritage.

Six semester hours in pre-professional courses in education.

Mentally Retarded

Completion of requirements in content courses for teachers in elementary schools.

Twelve semester hours in professional elementary education.

Three semester hours in a survey course in education for exceptional children.

Nine semester hours in courses directly related to teaching mentally retarded children.

Six semester hours in directed teaching which shall be in both this area of special education and the regular classroom.

UTAH

After September 1, 1961, the State of Utah will issue two certificates for teachers of special education classes for children with intellectual handicaps—a Provisional Certificate and a Professional Certificate.

An applicant for certification to teach special education classes for children with intellectual handicaps shall present evidence that he holds a general teacher's certificate for the level upon which he is employed except that either the elementary or secondary certificate is valid in grades seven through nine.

A. *Provisional Certificate*—Beginning September 1, 1961.

A provisional certificate for teachers of special education classes for children with intellectual handicaps will be issued upon the recommendation of a training institution to a teacher who has completed a minimum of fifteen quarter hours of credit in approved specialized training. This certificate is valid for two years and will be reissued upon completion of six quarter hours of credit in additional approved study until requirements for the professional certificate are met.

The minimum of fifteen quarter hours of approved specialized training required of all teachers qualifying for a provisional certificate in this area of special education shall include work in each of the following categories:

1. Introductory study of exceptional children and problems common to several areas of special education (Recommended minimum three quarter hours)

2. Study of biological, psychological and social aspects of mental deficiency (Recommended minimum three quarter hours)
3. Study of educational management of children with intellectual handicaps including: educational diagnosis, classroom organization, curriculum development, teaching procedures and materials (Recommended minimum six quarter hours)
4. Student teaching of children with intellectual handicaps in programs approved for this purpose (Laboratory experience or directed observation recommended by the university may be approved.) (Recommended minimum three quarter hours)

B. *Professional Certificate*—Beginning September 1, 1961.

A professional certificate for teachers of special education classes for children with intellectual handicaps will be issued upon the recommendation of a training institution to a teacher who has completed a minimum of thirty quarter hours of credit in approved specialized training. This certificate is valid for five years and will be reissued for five years upon completion of six quarter hours of credit in additional approved study.

The minimum of thirty quarter hours of approved specialized training required of all teachers qualifying for a professional certificate in this area of special education shall include work in each of the following categories:

1. Introductory study of exceptional children and problems common to several areas of special education (Recommended minimum three quarter hours)
2. Study of biological, psychological and social aspects

of mental deficiency (Recommended minimum nine quarter hours)

3. Study of educational management of children with intellectual handicaps including: educational diagnosis, classroom organization, curriculum development, teaching procedures and materials (Recommended minimum twelve quarter hours)
4. Student teaching of children with intellectual handicaps in programs approved for this purpose (Laboratory experience or directed observation recommended by the university may be approved.) (Recommended minimum six quarter hours)

VERMONT

To complete certification for teaching retarded children, a teacher must either have completed a program for the education of special teachers while working for her bachelor's degree or have completed a minimum of twelve semester hours of work in special education which shall include approved credit in special education methods, psychology of the exceptional child, special arts and crafts or occcupational education for retarded children. More detailed information about requirements can be obtained from the State Department of Education.

VIRGINIA

An applicant for endorsement to teach special classes of exceptional children must qualify for the Collegiate Professional Certificate.

Mentally Retarded	27 sem. hrs.
I. Required Credit	24 sem. hrs.

A minimum of three semester hours in each of the following:

A. Psychology of exceptional children
B. Survey of the education of exceptional children
C. Orientation in tests and measurements
D. Student teaching of mentally retarded children (Teachers who have met requirements in regular classroom under Area III will be required to submit three semester hours of credit in teaching mentally retarded children.) *
E. Speech problems of exceptional children
F. Characteristics of mentally retarded children
G. Education of mentally retarded children, with attention to methods and materials used in teaching children in the groups listed below:
    1. Primary age group (educable)
    2. Intermediate age group (educable)
    3. Secondary age group (educable)
    4. Severely retarded (trainable)
H. Vocational guidance and occupational adjustment of mentally retarded children, or arts and crafts

II. Related Areas 3 sem. hrs.
A. Mental health
B. General woodwork or industrial arts
C. Guidance

WASHINGTON

Basic Requirements Common to All Special Education Teachers

A. Valid Washington State Teaching Certificate (preferably elementary)
B. An understanding of exceptional children and of the field of special education
C. An understanding of the role of the special education

* May be credited for Student teaching under Area III.

teacher in the total program of educational, medical, psychological and welfare services in the community and sufficient background to receive and use confidential information from these sources

D. An understanding of the home, school and community relations of exceptional children
E. Counseling and guidance of handicapped
F. Student teaching with exceptional children

Basic Requirements for Teaching Mentally Retarded Should Include the General Areas Listed:

1. Education in problems of the mentally retarded
2. Curriculum and methods for teaching mentally retarded
3. Arts and crafts as related to mentally retarded
4. Student teaching of mentally retarded

WEST VIRGINIA

A. Each teacher employed in a special class for mentally retarded children must hold a valid West Virginia certificate for teaching.
B. Each teacher should have:
    1. Successful teaching experience with children of comparable age and/or ability levels
    2. Good background in child development
    3. Sympathetic understanding of and realistic attitude toward children who are mentally retarded
    4. Wide knowledge of instructional materials
    5. Ability to adapt materials and methods to meet the needs of pupils
    6. Familiarity with the services rendered by other people who contribute to the desirable adjustment and ultimate development of mentally retarded children

7. Ability to understand the implications of case histories, psychological reports, medical reports, and other such information in planning educational programs for children

C. Each teacher should take advantage of such special courses in this field as may be available.

WISCONSIN

A. Teachers of Mentally Retarded must meet the general state minimum standard of forty semester hours in liberal arts.

B. General Professional Training—eighteen hours required.

Required:

Child or adolescent development	Practice teaching with normals
Group tests and measurements	Curriculum planning

Electives:

Methods of instruction	Recreation
History of education	Guidance
Personality adjustment	Kindergarten–primary methods
Educational sociology	
Fundamentals of speech	Educational psychology
Audio-visual education	Others

Graduates of accredited colleges in the field of education which have been approved by the State Department, will have fulfilled the requirements of this section.

C. General Field of Special Education—six hours required.

Required:

Psychology of nature of the exceptional child

Electives:

Abnormal or clinical psychology
Individual mental testing (survey)
Guidance of exceptional children
Administration and supervision of speech education
Speech correction
Field work with the exceptional child
Home and community planning
Psychological appraisal of the physically handicapped
Teaching of physical education for the handicapped child
Health problems of the exceptional child

D. Area of Specialization—Mentally Retarded—twelve hours required.

Required:

Methods of teaching the mentally retarded
Practice teaching with the mentally retarded
Arts and crafts, or industrial arts, or home economics

Electives:

Remedial reading
Curriculum for the mentally retarded
Occupational information and guidance for the mentally retarded
Recreation for the mentally retarded
Music, education for the retarded
Art education for the mentally retarded
Introduction to mental retardation
Educational problems of the cerebral-palsied

Arrangements for substitution of other courses for those listed should be made upon direct application to the State Superintendent. Teachers of both educable and trainable service are required to meet state certification requirements. Degree holding and/or teachers holding an unlimited life license in the area of Mentally Retarded are to receive preference over non-degree teachers. In order to obtain a one-year permit to teach Mentally Retarded, an individual must satisfy a minimum of six hours in the area of the Education of the Mentally Retarded prior to beginning teaching in this field. Non-degree holding personnel are also required to work toward their next level of certification and may do this on an alternation year basis, completing six hours of Special Education one year and six hours toward their next level of certification the next year.

The Bureau strongly recommends the following sequence in completing Special Education requirements:

1. Workshop in education of mentally retarded
2. Psychology of exceptional child and arts and crafts
3. Electives in sections C and D

WYOMING

Special Education—Appropriate for Teaching the Educable Mentally Retarded

Requirements are:

Eligibility for a standard or professional teaching certificate twenty-four semester hours of upper division or graduate credit, including:

Ten semester hours in educational management of children with intellectual handicaps including such courses as Education of the mentally handicapped, Education of the slow learner, Curriculum development for the mentally retarded, Methods and materials for the mentally retarded or Special education, Laboratory practice, Mentally handicapped practicum.

Six semester hours in understanding the individual including such courses as Mental hygiene, Advanced psychology, Adjustment problems of the handicapped, Advanced tests and measurements, Advanced child psychology and Theory of learning, Psychological testing, Diagnosis of learning problems, Measurements of the handicapped, Psychology of individual differences.

Eight semester hours in the following areas with at least one course in each:

a. Introductory Study of Exceptional Children
   (Such courses as Introduction to Special Education, Psychology of Exceptional Children, Survey of Special Education, Education of Exceptional Children)
b. Supervision Placement and Guidance Techniques
   (Such courses as Supervision of Special Education, Administration of Special Education, Counseling Parents, Workshop for Rehabilitation of the Mentally Retarded, Workshop in Guidance Techniques for the Mentally Retarded, Advanced Counseling, Community Resources for Exceptional Children, Occupational Information for the Mentally Retarded)
c. Related Areas
   (Such courses as Organic Disorders of Speech, Introduction to Speech Correction, Remedial Reading, Remedial and Diagnostic Techniques, Arts and Crafts for the Mentally Retarded)

The authors gratefully acknowledge permission of the National Association for Retarded Children for use of material used in the development of this chapter.

CHAPTER **7**

Financial Assistance

Numerous resources are available to persons in need of financial assistance during the course of their professional training in the field of education of the mentally retarded. Assistance in the form of scholarships and loans is reported below under the following headings: Assistance from Colleges and Universities; Assistance from the Federal Government and Assistance from State Agencies.

Assistance from Colleges and Universities

General Scholarships–Undergraduate

A major source of financial assistance in the field of education is found in the general scholarship and loan services extended by institutions in higher learning. Many colleges have scholarships which remain undistributed because no one requests this aid. Such general scholarships are available to students regardless of their major area of study. Persons desiring training in the area of education of the mentally retarded are eligible for such scholarships. In 1957 the U. S. Office of Education reported 1,562 institutions of higher learning offering 237,370 scholarships. At that time undergraduate scholarships averaged $277. Those persons desiring such general scholarship or loan assistance should write directly to the college or university of their choice for further information.

Undergraduate Scholarships in Mental Retardation

The following institutions are known to offer scholarships in the field of mental retardation:

Arizona State University:	One $350 scholarship for teachers of the mentally retarded.
University of Kentucky:	43 summer scholarships are available for teachers of retarded children.
University of Louisville:	35 summer scholarships are available for teachers of retarded children.

The following publications will be of value:

1. Scholarships and Fellowships—a selected Bibliography, Offices of Education Bulletin 1957, No. 7, Government Printing Office, Washington 25, D.C. (15¢)
2. Financial Aid for College Students: Undergraduate, Office of Education Bulletin 1957, No. 18, Government Printing Office, Washington 25, D.C. ($1.00)

Assistance from the Federal Government

The National Defense Student Loan Program *

Eligibility

Since each participating institution is responsible for determining the eligibility of a candidate for a loan, a prospective borrower must apply for loan assistance to the financial aid office of the college of his choice. The law requires that each borrower be a full-time undergraduate or graduate student, that he be in need of the amount of his loan to pursue his courses of study, and that he be, in the opinion of his institution, capable of maintaining good standing in his chosen courses of study. The law further provides that special consideration in the selection of loan recipients be given to students (a) with a superior academic background who express a desire to teach in elementary or secondary schools, or (b) whose academic background indicates a superior capacity or preparation in science, mathematics, engineering, or a modern foreign language.

Terms of Loan

The student may borrow for college expenses in one year a sum not exceeding $1,000 and, during his entire course in higher education, a sum not exceeding $5,000. (The national average of the annual loan per student has been about $500.) The borrower must sign a note for his loan. The repayment period of the loan begins one year after he completes his full-time course work and then extends over a ten-year period. Interest at 3 percent per year begins to accrue at the beginning of the repay-

* U.S. Office of Education—*The National Defense Student Loan Program,* Washington, D.C.: U.S. Government Printing Office, 1962.

ment period. During periods of service in the Armed Forces or the Peace Corps (up to a total of three years) and during periods of full-time attendance at an accredited institution of higher education, no interest will accrue and no repayment is required. The borrower's obligation to repay his loan is to be canceled in the event of his death or permanent and total disability.

Forgiveness Clause for Public School Teachers

If the borrower becomes a full-time teacher in a public elementary or secondary school, a maximum of 50 percent of the loan (plus interest) may be canceled at the rate of 10 percent for each year of teaching.

For Further Information

A high school student interested in knowing about the National Defense Student Loan Program should consult his principal or guidance counselor and the appropriate official of the participating college in which he expects to be enrolled. For the prospective student this official will usually be the Director of Admissions.

A student already enrolled in a participating college or university should consult the official in charge of student financial aid.

Loan application forms should be secured from the appropriate official of the participating institution. They are not available from the United States Office of Education.

The Grant Program for the Preparation of Professional Personnel in the Education of Handicapped

In 1964, 103 colleges and universities received federal funds to provide scholarships and senior traineeships to prepare teachers and supervisors of teachers of the mentally retarded. The colleges receiving these grants are listed below. Interested persons should write directly to the college of their choice.

ALABAMA
Auburn University, Auburn
University of Alabama, University

ARIZONA
Arizona State University, Tempe
University of Arizona, Tucson

ARKANSAS
Arkansas State Teachers College, Conway

CALIFORNIA
California State College, Los Angeles
San Francisco State College, San Francisco
University of Southern California, Los Angeles

COLORADO
Colorado State College, Greeley
University of Denver, Denver

CONNECTICUT
Saint Joseph College, West Hartford
Southern Connecticut State College, New Haven

WASHINGTON, D.C.
Catholic University of America
George Washington University

FLORIDA
Florida State University, Tallahassee
University of Florida, Gainesville
University of Miami, Coral Gables
University of Southern Florida, Tampa

GEORGIA
University of Georgia, Athens

IDAHO
- Idaho State University, Pocatello

ILLINOIS
- Illinois State University, Normal
- Southern Illinois University, Carbondale
- University of Illinois, Urbana

INDIANA
- Ball State Teachers College, Muncie
- Indiana State College, Terre Haute
- Indiana University, Bloomington

IOWA
- Drake University, Des Moines
- State College of Iowa, Cedar Falls
- State University of Iowa, Iowa City

KANSAS
- Kansas State Teachers College, Emporia
- University of Kansas, Lawrence

KENTUCKY
- University of Kentucky, Lexington

MARYLAND
- Coppin State College, Baltimore
- University of Maryland, College Park

MASSACHUSETTS
- Boston College, Chestnut Hill
- Boston University, Boston

MICHIGAN
- Eastern Michigan University, Ypsilanti
- Michigan State University, East Lansing
- University of Michigan, Ann Arbor
- Wayne State University, Detroit
- Western Michigan University, Kalamazoo

MINNESOTA
- Mankato State College, Mankato

Moorhead State College, Moorhead
St. Cloud State College, St. Cloud
University of Minnesota, Minneapolis

MISSISSIPPI
University of Mississippi, University
University of Southern Mississippi, Hattiesburg

MISSOURI
St. Louis University, St. Louis

MONTANA
Eastern Montana College of Education, Billings

NEBRASKA
Kearney State College, Kearney
University of Nebraska, Lincoln

NEW JERSEY
Jersey City State College, Jersey City
Newark State College, Union
Trenton State College, Trenton

NEW YORK
Fordham University, Bronx
New York University, New York
State University College at Buffalo, Buffalo
State University College at Geneseo, Geneseo
Syracuse University, Syracuse
Teachers College, Columbia University, New York
Yeshiva University, New York

NORTH CAROLINA
University of North Carolina, Chapel Hill
Western Carolina College, Cullowhee

NORTH DAKOTA
Minot State College, Minot
University of North Dakota, Grand Forks

OHIO
Bowling Green State University, Bowling Green
Kent State University, Kent

Ohio State University, Columbus
University of Cincinnati, Cincinnati

OKLAHOMA

Central State College, Edmond

OREGON

University of Oregon, Eugene

PENNSYLVANIA

Bloomsburg State College, Bloomsburg
Clarion State College, Clarion
Duquesne University, Pittsburgh
Marywood College, Scranton
Millersville State College, Millersville
Pennsylvania State University, University Park
University of Pittsburgh, Pittsburgh

RHODE ISLAND

Rhode Island College, Providence

SOUTH CAROLINA

Columbia College, Columbia
South Carolina State College, Orangeburg
University of South Carolina, Columbia

SOUTH DAKOTA

University of South Dakota, Vermillion

TENNESSEE

George Peabody College for Teachers, Nashville
University of Tennessee, Knoxville

TEXAS

East Texas State College, Commerce
Hardin-Simmons University, Abilene
Incarnate Word College, San Antonio
Lamar State College of Technology, Beaumont
Texas Woman's University, Denton
University of Houston, Houston
University of Texas, Austin

UTAH

Utah State University, Logan

VIRGINIA

University of Virginia, Charlottesville
Virginia State College, Petersburg

WASHINGTON

University of Washington, Seattle
Western Washington State College, Bellingham

WEST VIRGINIA

Marshall University, Huntington

WISCONSIN

Cardinal Stritch College, Milwaukee
University of Wisconsin, Madison
University of Wisconsin-Milwaukee, Milwaukee
Wisconsin State College-Eau Claire, Eau Claire
Wisconsin State College-Oshkosh, Oshkosh

WYOMING

University of Wyoming, Laramie

Assistance from State Agencies

General Teacher Education

More than thirty states have scholarships available in teacher education, and some states have special scholarships available for their teachers in the area of mental retardation.

Teachers of the Mentally Retarded

The following states offer scholarship assistance for the preparation of teachers of the mentally retarded:

Arkansas
Louisiana
Massachusetts
New York
Oregon

California, Florida and Rhode Island have scholarships in special education.

Selected References

Angel, Juvenal. *National Register of Scholarships and Fellowships*. Vol. I and II. New York: World Trade Academy Press, 1959.

Brownstein, Weiner and Kaplan. *You Can Win A Scholarship*. New York: Baron's Educational Series, Inc., 1958.

Feingold, N. S. *Scholarships, Fellowships and Loans*. Boston: Bellman Publishing Company, Inc., 1957.

Lovejoy, C. E. and T. Jones. *College Scholarship Guide*. New York: Simon and Schuster, 1957.

Need a Lift–Education Opportunities. Information Service, The American Legion, P.O. Box 1055, Indianapolis 6, Indiana.

Office of Education. *National Defense Graduate Fellowships: Graduate Programs, 1963-64*. Washington, D.C.: U.S. Government Printing Office, 1963.

Scholarships and Fellowships–A Selected Bibliography. U.S. Department of Health, Education and Welfare, Bulletin 1957, No. 7. (Available from the Supt. of Documents, Washington 25, D.C.–15¢.)

Brochure on PL 85-926. *The Graduate Fellowship Program*. Bulletin OE-35001. Office of Education, Washington, D.C. (Free).

Appendix

Colleges and Universities Offering an Undergraduate Sequence of Courses in Education of the Mentally Retarded

State	*Name and Address*	*Extent to Which State Certification Requirements Are Met*	*When Courses Offered* *
Alabama			
	Alabama Agricultural and Mechanical College, Normal	—	S
	Auburn University, Auburn	All	R & S
	Troy State College, Troy	Part	S
	Tuskegee Institute, Tuskegee	All	S
	University of Alabama, University	All	R & S
Arizona			
	Arizona State University, Tempe	All	R & S
	University of Arizona, Tucson	All	R & S
Arkansas			
	Arkansas State College, State College	All	R & S

* R—Regular session; S—Summer session.

State	*Name and Address*	*Extent to Which State Certification Requirements Are Met*	*When Courses Offered*
	Arkansas State Teachers College, Conway	All	S
California			
	Chapman College, Orange	All	R & S
	Chico State College, Chico	All	S
	Fresno State College, Fresno	All	R & S
	Humboldt State College, Arcata	Part	R & S
	Long Beach State College, Long Beach	All	R & S
	Los Angeles State College, Los Angeles	All	R & S
	Pepperdine College, Los Angeles	All	R & S
	Sacramento State College, Sacramento	All	R & S
	San Diego State College, San Diego	All	R & S
	San Fernando Valley State College, Northride	All	R & S
	San Francisco State College, San Francisco	All	R & S
	San Jose State College, San Jose	Part	R & S
	University of the Pacific, Stockton	All	R & S
	University of Southern California, Los Angeles	Part	R & S
Colorado			
	Colorado State College, Greeley	All	R & S
	University of Denver, Denver	All	R & S
Connecticut			
	Southern Connecticut State College, New Haven	All	R & S
	University of Connecticut, Storrs	All	R & S

State	*Name and Address*	*Extent to Which State Certification Requirements Are Met*	*When Courses Offered*
	University of Hartford Hillyer College, Hartford	All	R & S
Florida			
	Florida Agricultural and Mechanical University, Tallahassee	All	S
	Florida Normal and Industrial Memorial College, St. Augustine	Part	S
	Florida State University, Tallahassee	All	R & S
	University of Florida, Gainesville	All	R & S
	University of Miami, Coral Gables	All	R & S
Georgia			
	Albany State College, Albany	Part	S
	Shorter College, Rome	All	R & S
	University of Georgia, Athens	All	R & S
Hawaii			
	University of Hawaii, Honolulu	All	R & S
Idaho			
	Idaho State College, Pocatello	All	R & S
Illinois			
	Chicago Teachers College, Chicago	All	R & S
	Illinois State Normal University, Normal	All	R & S
	MacMurray College, Jacksonville	All	R & S
	Northern Illinois University, DeKalb	All	R & S
	Southern Illinois University, Carbondale	All	R & S
	Southern Illinois University, Edwardsville	All	R & S

State	Name and Address	Extent to Which State Certification Requirements Are Met	When Courses Offered
	University of Illinois, Urbana	All	R & S
Indiana			
	Ball State Teachers College, Muncie	All	R & S
	Indiana State College, Terre Haute	All	R & S
	Indiana University, Bloomington	All	R & S
	Purdue University, Lafayette	All	R
Iowa			
	State College of Iowa, Cedar Falls	All	R & S
	State University of Iowa, Iowa City	All	R & S
	Upper Iowa University, Fayette	Part	R & S
Kansas			
	Kansas State Teachers College of Pittsburgh, Pittsburgh	All	R & S
	Kansas State Teachers College, Emporia	All	R & S
	University of Kansas, Lawrence	All	R & S
Kentucky			
	Brescia College, Owensboro	All	S
	University of Kentucky, Lexington	All	R & S
	University of Louisville, Louisville	All	R & S
Louisiana			
	Louisiana Polytechnic Institute, Ruston	All	R & S
	Louisiana State University & Agricultural & Mechanical College, Baton Rouge	All	R & S
	McNeese State College, Lake Charles	All	R & S

State	Name and Address	*Extent to Which State Certification Requirements Are Met*	*When Courses Offered*
	Northeast Louisiana State College, Monroe	All	R & S
	Northwestern State College of Louisiana, Natchitoches	All	R & S
	St. Mary's Dominican College, New Orleans	Part	R & S
	Southern University and Agricultural and Mechanical College, Baton Rouge	All	R & S
	The University of Southwestern Louisiana, Lafayette	All	R & S
Maine			
	Farmington State Teachers College, Farmington	All	R & S
Maryland			
	University of Maryland, College Park	All	R & S
Massachusetts			
	Boston College, Chestnut Hill	All	R
	Boston University, Boston	All	R & S
	Lesley College, Cambridge	All	R & S
	Springfield College, Springfield	Part	R & S
	State College at Fitchburgh, Fitchburgh	All	R & S
Michigan			
	Central Michigan University, Mt. Pleasant	All	R & S
	Eastern Michigan College, Ypsilanti	All	R & S
	Marygrove College, Detroit	All	R & S

State	Name and Address	Extent to Which State Certification Requirements Are Met	When Courses Offered
	Michigan State University, E. Lansing	All	R & S
	Northern Michigan College, Marquette	All	R & S
	The University of Michigan, Ann Arbor	All	R & S
	Wayne State University, Detroit	All	R & S
	Western Michigan University, Kalamazoo	All	R & S
Minnesota			
	Mankato State College, Mankato	All	R & S
	Moorhead State College, Moorhead	All	R & S
	St. Cloud State College, St. Cloud	All	R & S
	University of Minnesota, Minneapolis	All	R & S
Mississippi			
	University of Mississippi, University	Part	R & S
	University of Southern Mississippi, Hattiesburg	All	R & S
Missouri			
	Central Missouri State College, Warrensburg	All	R & S
	Culver-Stockton College, Canton	Part	R & S
	Lincoln University, Jefferson City	Part	S
	Northeast Missouri State Teachers College, Kirksville	All	R & S
	St. Louis University, St. Louis		
	University of Kansas City, Kansas City	Part	R & S

State	Name and Address	Extent to Which State Certification Requirements Are Met	When Courses Offered
	Washington University, St. Louis	All	R & S
Montana			
	Eastern Montana College of Education, Billings	All	R & S
Nebraska			
	Nebraska State Teachers College, Wayne	All	R & S
	Municipal University of Omaha, Omaha	All	R & S
	Nebraska State Teachers College, Kearney	All	R & S
Nevada			
	University of Nevada, Reno	All	R & S
New Hampshire			
	Keene Teachers College, Keene	All	R & S
New Jersey			
	Glassboro State College, Glassboro	All	R & S
	Jersey City State College, Jersey City	All	R & S
	Newark State College, Newark	All	R & S
	Trenton State College, Trenton	All	R & S
New Mexico			
	Eastern New Mexico University, Portals	All	S
	New Mexico Western College, Silver City	All	R & S
	University of New Mexico, Albuquerque	All	R & S
New York			
	City College, New York	All	R & S

State	*Name and Address*	*Extent to Which State Certification Requirements Are Met*	*When Courses Offered*
	College of Education at Buffalo, Buffalo	All	R & S
	College of Education at Geneseo, Geneseo	All	R & S
	Syracuse University, Syracuse	Part	R & S
North Carolina			
	East Carolina College, Greenville	All	R & S
North Dakota			
	State Teachers College, Minot	All	R & S
	University of North Dakota, Grand Forks	All	R & S
Ohio			
	Kent State University, Kent	All	R & S
	Ohio State University, Columbus	All	R & S
	Ohio University, Athens	All	R & S
	University of Cincinnati, Cincinnati	All	R & S
	University of Dayton, Dayton	Part	R & S
Oklahoma			
	Central State College, Edmond	All	R & S
	Oklahoma State University of Agriculture & Applied Science, Stillwater	Part	R & S
	University of Oklahoma, Norman	All	R & S
	University of Tulsa, Tulsa	All	R & S
Pennsylvania			
	Bloomsburg State College, Bloomsburg	All	R & S
	California State College, California	All	R & S
	Cheyney State College, Cheyney	All	R & S

State	*Name and Address*	*Extent to Which State Certification Requirements Are Met*	*When Courses Offered*
	Clarion State College, Clarion	All	R & S
	College of Misericordia, Dallas	All	R & S
	Edinboro State College, Edinboro	All	R & S
	Indiana State College, Indiana	All	R & S
	Kutztown State College, Kutztown	All	R & S
	Lock Haven State College, Lock Haven	Part	R & S
	Mansfield State College, Mansfield	Part	R & S
	Millersville State College, Millersville	All	R & S
	Pennsylvania State University, University Park	All	R & S
	Shippensburg State College, Shippensburg	All	R & S
	Temple University, Philadelphia	All	R & S
	University of Scranton, Scranton	Part	R & S
	West Chester State College, West Chester	Part	R & S
Rhode Island			
	Rhode Island College, Providence	All	R & S
South Carolina			
	University of South Carolina, Columbia	All	R & S
South Dakota			
	Black Hills Teachers College, Spearfish	Part	S
	Northern State Teachers College, Aberdeen	All	R & S
	State University of South Dakota, Vermillion	All	S

State	Name and Address	Extent to Which State Certification Requirements Are Met	When Courses Offered
Tennessee			
	East Tennessee State College, Johnson City	All	R & S
	George Peabody College for Teachers, Nashville	All	R & S
	Memphis State University, Memphis	All	R & S
	Tennessee Agricultural & Industrial State University, Nashville	All	R & S
Texas			
	Baylor University, Waco	All	R & S
	Incarnate Word College, San Antonio	All	R & S
	Lamar State College of Technology, Beaumont	All	R & S
	Pan American College, Edinburg	All	R & S
	Southwest Texas State College, San Marcos	All	R & S
	Stephen F. Austin State College, Nacogdoches	All	S
	Texas College of Arts and Industries, Kingsville	All	S
	University of Houston, Houston	All	R & S
	University of Texas, Austin	All	R & S
	West Texas State College, Canyon	All	R & S
	Wiley College, Marshall	All	R & S
Utah			
	Utah State University of Agriculture & Applied Science, Logan	All	R & S

State	*Name and Address*	*Extent to Which State Certification Requirements Are Met*	*When Courses Offered*
Virginia			
	University of Virginia, Charlottesville	Part	R & S
	Virginia State College, Petersburg	All	R & S
Washington			
	Central Washington State College, Ellensburg	All	R & S
	Eastern Washington State College, Cheney	All	R & S
	University of Washington, Seattle	All	R & S
W. Virginia			
	Marshall University, Huntington	All	R & S
Wisconsin			
	The Cardinal Stritch College, Milwaukee	All	S
	University of Wisconsin, Milwaukee	All	R & S
	Wisconsin State College, Eau Claire	All	R & S
	Wisconsin State College & Institute of Technology, Oshkosh	All	S
Wyoming			
	University of Wyoming, Laramie	Part	R & S

Bibliography

The references below were selected because of their readability and ease of use. There are of course many other sources; see the *Bibliography of World Literature on Mental Retardation* for a complete listing.

General

National Association for Retarded Children, *Facts on Mental Retardation,* available from *NARC,* 386 Park Ave., So., New York, New York 10016.

About Becoming a Teacher

Charney, Leon and LaCrosse, Edward, *Opportunities for Professional Preparation in the Field of Education of Mentally Retarded Children,* available from *NARC,* 386 Park Ave., So., New York, New York 10016—$1.00.

NARC—Make Teaching Retarded Children Your Career, available from *NARC*—single copies, free.

About Teaching the Retarded

Hill, Margaret, *The Extra-Special Room,* Little Brown and Company, Inc., 1962—$3.50.

About Retarded Children and Their Families

Kirk, Samuel, Karnes, Merle and Kirk, Winifred, *You and Your Retarded Child,* The Macmillan Co., 1958—$4.00.

Murray, Dorothy, *Stevie's Story,* Brethren Publishing House, 1956 —$1.00.

INDEX

Index